ILLUSTRATED BOOK OF

◈ GREAT ◈

ADVENTURES

Meriwether Lewis knows that he is in trouble when his ammunition runs out
and he comes face to face with an angry bear in "A Grizzly Attack."

ILLUSTRATED BOOK OF

⬡ GREAT ⬡

ADVENTURES

Real-life tales of danger and daring

Written by
RICHARD PLATT

Illustrated by
GEORGE SHARP
WITH MALCOLM CHANDLER,
ROB McCAIG, AND
ANDREW WHEATCROFT

A DK PUBLISHING BOOK
www.dk.com

A DK PUBLISHING BOOK
www.dk.com

Project Editor Mary Atkinson

Art Editors Sarah Ponder,
Peter Radcliffe

Senior Editor Scarlett O'Hara

Senior Managing Editor Linda Martin

Senior Managing Art Editor Julia Harris

DTP Designers Almudena Díaz,
Andrew O'Brien

Researcher Robert Graham

Production Ruth Cobb, Lisa Moss

US Editors Lilan Patri, Connie Robinson

First American Edition, 1999
2 4 6 8 10 9 7 5 3 1

Published in the United States by
DK Publishing, Inc.
95 Madison Avenue
New York, New York 10016

Published in Great Britain by Dorling Kindersley Limited

Library of Congress Cataloging-in-Publication Data

DK Illustrated book of great adventures. -- 1st American ed.
          p.   cm.
Includes index.
Summary: Presents the activities and accomplishments of great adventurers
throughout history, including the Viking explorer Leif Eriksson and astronaut
Neil Armstrong.
ISBN 0-7894-4461-5
1. Adventure and adventurers--Juvenile literature. [1. Adventure and adventurers.]
I. Title: Great adventures.
G525.D54 1999
910'.92'2--dc21
                                                    98-49574
                                                      CIP
                                                      AC

Color reproduction by Bright Arts in Singapore
Printed and bound by Graphicom in Italy

CONTENTS

A trap was laid for Cortés and his Spanish army in "The Siege of Tenochtitlán."

Titus Oates disappears into the whirling snow in "Race to the South Pole."

Australian Aborigines try to help Burke and Wills in "The Fatal Desert Crossing."

INTRODUCTION

WHAT IS IT that makes an adventurer? For some, it's a restless urge to wander. For others, it's a desire to be famous, to get rich quick, or to conquer an empire. For a few, it's just the feeling of being an outsider with nothing left to lose. Above all, though, it's a hunger for excitement and for life itself.

Most of us are thrilled and inspired by an adventurer's tale. Stories of exploring the unknown have always conjured up images of exotic cities, wild creatures, and fabulous riches—the very things that the adventurers of old discovered.

In the 15th century, when Columbus and other explorers returned triumphant from the West, many Europeans became aware of the American continent for the first time. The adventurers told of its peoples, its vast and beautiful landscapes populated by grizzly bears, buffaloes, and jaguars; they brought back new foods, such as spices, chocolate, and the potato, and they told stories of finding gold and precious gems. In fact, the tales must have fulfilled everyone's wildest dreams of adventure and discovery.

Adventurers have always taken great risks. Fear of wild animals, bandits, storms, and most of all, fear of the unknown have never deterred them. Today's adventurers climb high mountains, explore the frozen poles, and take the most dangerous and exciting risk of all, exploring the unknown worlds of outer space.

DIFFERENT TYPES OF ADVENTURER

Not all the adventurers in this book were explorers. Some made daring escapes from prison, others were rebels or outlaws. Some were even reckless criminals who destroyed anything or anyone in their way. Blackbeard the pirate, for example, was a cruel and merciless villain (see pp. 42–45).

There are also stories of adventurers who were once seen as heroes, but whose acts can now seem cruel. For instance, many people now believe that Hernán Cortés and his soldiers were wrong to kill so many Aztecs and steal their property when they conquered Mexico for Spain in the 16th century (see pp. 28–31). Yet 100 years ago, they were seen as clever and courageous.

Most of the stories in this book are about men. This doesn't mean that men make better adventurers than women! Many of the adventurers lived in times when women and men didn't have equal rights. Only the bravest women dared rebel against these rules. Also, most historians (people who study and write about the past) used to be men, and they recorded history from a man's point of view. We will never know how many female adventurers have been forgotten.

ARE THE STORIES TRUE?

News reporters and television cameras now record the epic feats of many adventurers. However, photography and film are recent inventions. In the past, adventurers were unable to bring back this kind of proof of where they'd been.

Many early adventurers couldn't write; instead they repeated their tales to anyone who would listen. It's likely that those who passed on the tales invented extra details to make them even

more exciting. So how do we know if a story is true?

Occasionally, there is evidence that an adventurer from ancient times did exist. For instance, in 1963, scientists dug up 1,000-year-old Viking objects in Newfoundland, Canada. This suggests that Vikings—perhaps even "Lucky" Leif Eriksson (see pp. 12–13)—really did visit America five centuries before Christopher Columbus (see pp. 20–23).

More often, though, there is no way to tell if a story is true or not. We just have to take the storyteller's word for it—and enjoy the tale. Good or bad, real or invented, the one thing all adventurers have in common is bravery.

It's hard not to envy them their courage and to respect their determination to be bolder, brasher, better, or even "badder" than all their rivals. So read on—and maybe some of their adventurous spirit will rub off on you!

Richard Platt

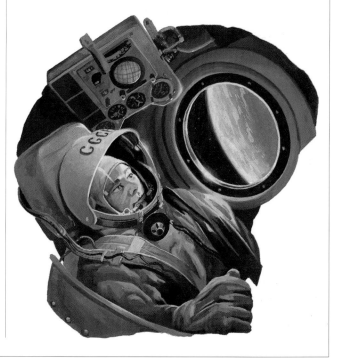

DISCOVERY, CONQUEST, AND LOOT

"IT'S IMPOSSIBLE!" To an adventurer these words are not a warning, but a challenge. Marching an army across a high mountain range was "impossible," but Carthaginian general Hannibal tried it anyway. He even took his war elephants on the arduous journey. Sailing from Europe to India was "impossible," until Portuguese navigator Vasco da Gama led his fleet around Africa's southern tip.

In the stories that follow, legendary adventurers set off on all sorts of voyages into the unknown—and many return to brag about their "impossible" successes. There are the famous explorers who discovered the lands they called the New World. And there are also some frightening rogues whose impossibly daring pranks shocked and impressed the world.

Blackbeard struck terror into his victims—and his crew—in "Blackbeard the Pirate."

HANNIBAL CROSSES THE ALPS

The story so far...

The Carthaginians from North Africa had lost the first war against the Romans (264–241 BC). Now Roman ships protected Italy's coast. So the Carthaginian general, Hannibal, plotted a land attack. He would invade Italy's unguarded northern border with 40,000 troops and 37 elephants. In May 218 BC, Hannibal and his army set out from southern Spain.

THE MIGHTY GENERAL
The son of a great Carthaginian general, Hannibal Barca (247–183/1 BC), became one of the greatest military commanders of the ancient world. At just 26 years old, he was chosen by the powerful Carthaginian army as their leader. Three years later, he led his soldiers against Rome.

HANNIBAL'S ROUTE
Hannibal marched his loyal troops through Spain and southern France to reach Italy. When the long war ended, he returned to Carthage by sea.

THE MIGHTY RIVER RHÔNE ALMOST STOPPED Hannibal's advance. A friendly ferryman took some soldiers across; most paddled on makeshift canoes or rafts, and their horses swam behind. But the elephants, Hannibal's vital weapons of terror, refused to go near the water.

Then Hannibal had an ingenious idea.

"Make huge rafts," he ordered his engineers. "Cover them with packed earth, and moor them at the water's edge."

The simple trick worked. Mistaking the rafts for dry land, the huge beasts lumbered aboard. However, when the rafts left the bank, the elephants panicked. One raft rocked and tilted. With an enormous splash, the terrified elephants fell trumpeting into the muddy water. They were as resourceful as their general, though. They completed the crossing underwater, breathing through their trunks as a skin diver sucks air through a snorkel!

Hannibal rested his troops on the far bank. Now only the Alps kept him out of Italy. But his scouts brought bad news. An enormous Roman army was in Marseille, just four days' march to the south. There was no time to lose. By dawn, Hannibal's troops were on their way north.

Hannibal's movements amazed Scipio, the leader of the Roman forces. The news that Hannibal had turned north could mean only one thing. He was preparing to cross the Alps. It was impossible! The army would have to march about 250 miles (400 kilometers) and cross a mountain range. No army had ever crossed the Alps, let alone with elephants!

Scipio acted swiftly. He left Marseille on the first boat. If the Carthaginians survived the Alpine crossing, a vast Roman army would be waiting for them in Italy.

As Scipio sailed for Italy, Hannibal was already in the alpine foothills. He had hoped to reach the Alps in summer, but fighting in Spain had delayed him. Now his shivering African troops scrambled up the steep slopes in autumn rain and fog.

Their problems had only just begun. As they climbed higher, the march became a deadly ordeal. Betrayed by local guides, the Carthaginians walked into a trap. When the troops entered a gorge, the Gauls, Rome's allies, attacked them from behind and rolled rocks onto them from high above.

Hannibal's army was trapped. On one side rose a sheer cliff; on the other side was a dizzy drop into a deep ravine. They had nowhere to hide, and they could neither advance nor retreat. Frightened horses shied and backed down the path, forcing those behind them over the edge to certain death.

But Hannibal's troops fought off the ambush with such determination that the Gauls eventually withdrew. At last, after nine days' march uphill, Hannibal found a pass, a low point between the snow-covered peaks, where his army could cross.

There, on the threshold of Italy, he addressed his troops. The mists cleared briefly, revealing the plains of Italy far below. Hannibal pointed into the distance.

"Rome is in that direction. Just one battle, maybe two, and we shall be masters of the city," he said.

Hannibal's speech cheered his men, but their hardships were not over yet. Deep snow slowed their descent and kept the animals from grazing. A landslide had swept away part of the path, leaving a huge boulder in their way. While hungry elephants stamped their feet impatiently, Hannibal's engineers heaped wood on the boulder and set fire to it. Soon the rock was red hot. Throwing vinegar on it shattered the rock into a thousand pieces.

Troops, horses, and elephants filed through the gap and marched into Italy to do battle with Scipio's Roman army. Hannibal's "impossible" march had taken only two weeks.

IN THE YEARS THAT FOLLOWED…

Hannibal paid a high price for his epic journey. More than half his troops died. Though the elephants survived the crossing, the freezing Italian winter killed all but one. Riding on the survivor's back, Hannibal went on to crush the Roman army at the battle of Cannae in 216 BC. But despite fighting in Italy for 15 years, Hannibal could not defeat the Romans, and he returned to Africa in 203 BC.

LUCKY LEIF

LEIF ERIKSSON THUMPED his massive fist on the bench.

"Father! You must lead us! We shall discover a new land. I've bought Bjarni's boat and hired a crew. We sail on tomorrow's tide."

"I can't go, Leif! I'm too old," complained Erik the Red. "My days of discovering new lands are over. You must lead this trip yourself."

For a moment, Leif hesitated. It wasn't the journey that he feared; he was prepared for the hardships of the sea. What frightened him were the unknown dangers of a new world beyond the sunset. But Leif's curiosity overcame his fear, and soon his sleek longboat was slicing through the Atlantic spray.

At first, Leif sailed north along Greenland's coast. But after several days, he turned west, out of sight of land. He had neither a map nor a compass. Instead, his crew steered by the sun and stars, the wind, and the ocean currents.

The crossing was a cold, exhausting ordeal. Icy polar winds blew them along quickly but cut through the crew members' thick clothing, chilling them to the bone.

The powerful ocean waves tugged and tore at the thin hull of the *knarr* (cargo ship), opening the seams so that the sea leaked in though a thousand tiny cracks. Bailing went on day and night as the crew fought the rising water.

After just two days, the lookout spotted a snowy coastline ahead. Leif stared from the prow, the sea wind matting his ginger-colored beard.

"It's a land of just rock and ice," he called out.

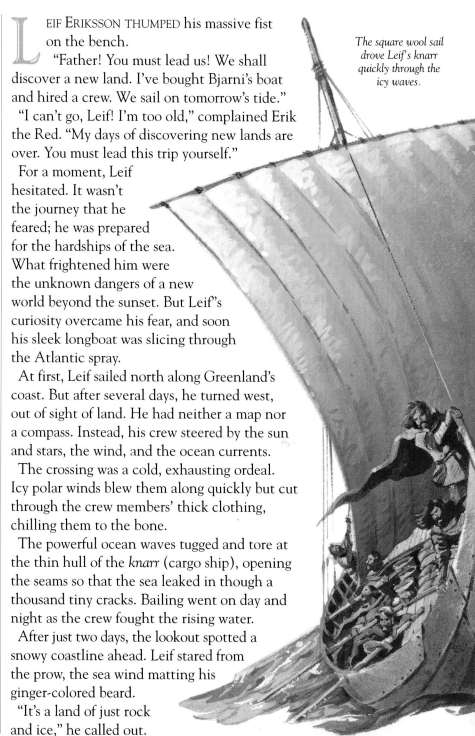

The square wool sail drove Leif's knarr quickly through the icy waves.

The story so far…

Some time before AD 1000, Viking Bjarni Herolfsson was sailing to Greenland when a storm blew his ship off course to the west of the island. Before sailing home, he sighted several strange new lands. He sailed along their coasts but did not set foot on them. When he and his crew eventually anchored in Greenland, their exploit created a great deal of excitement. Everyone talked about voyaging west to discover new lands.

VIKING HERO

Leif Eriksson (AD 970–1024) lived so long ago that we know very little about him, although it is thought that he was born in Greenland. In AD 1000, Leif sailed to Norway, where he converted to Christianity. He promised the king of Norway that he would spread Christianity to Greenland when he returned. Leif's father, Erik the Red, was also an explorer. He came from the Viking settlement in Iceland and had led the Viking colonization of Greenland.

When they reached shallower water, they anchored and went ashore. Leif was right: Towering glaciers had scraped off the soil and worn smooth the rock beneath. Even a determined Viking could not farm this desolate land. But Leif just laughed at his men's disappointment.

"At least we landed. Bjarni didn't even manage that. We'll call this 'Flat Stone Land' and sail on," he told them. But they didn't have to sail far. Soon they spied a long, low coastline covered with forest. They anchored at a beach of glittering white sand and explored briefly.

"Let's call this 'Forest Land,'" said Leif as they rowed back to the ship. With new enthusiasm, they sailed on, and two days later, they saw what they were looking for. Through the sea mist, a beautiful wooded coastline appeared with gently rolling hills behind it. Leif knew this was the land that Bjarni had described. His men could scarcely contain their excitement. They explored the country and found good pastureland and many large trees. Salmon jumped in the crystal-clear rivers. Compared with bleak, treeless Greenland, it was paradise. They were so enchanted that they built houses out of turf and wood and planned to spend the winter there.

One day, Leif's friend Tyrkir returned from hunting, full of excitement. "I've discovered vines and grapes!" he called out. " Now we can make wine." They weren't really grapes, only a kind of berry, but to the Vikings they symbolized the richness of this newly discovered land. When spring came, they set off for Greenland with a valuable cargo of timber and "grapes."

Their adventure was not quite over, however.

On the way, Leif's sharp eyes spotted the survivors of a wreck, stranded on rocks. He picked up the 15 mariners, earning himself a new nickname—Leif the Lucky.

IN THE YEARS THAT FOLLOWED…

Leif became famous in Greenland. The story of his pioneering journey was retold to each generation. The Viking storytellers used the name Leif had given the new land—Vinland—chosen because of the vines that grew there. Today, the land is called Newfoundland.

Leif and his crew built houses to keep themselves warm and safe from wild animals over the winter.

Viking weather vane

THE VIKING AGE
The Vikings settled much of Scandinavia 11 centuries ago. Skilled in iron working and the building and sailing of ships, they prospered on the coasts as well as inland. Some became pirates, and others went in search of new lands to farm.

→ Eric the Red's journey
→ Leif Eriksson's journey

ISLAND-HOPPING
Brave and inquisitive Vikings traveled 2,300 miles (3,700 kilometers) from their homeland to reach America. They did it by sailing from island to island across the north Atlantic. On their voyages, Leif and his father were never more than 115 miles (185 kilometers) from land.

THE COURT OF KUBLAI KHAN

The story so far...

Marco Polo was 17 years old when he set off from his home in Venice, Italy, hoping to trade in exotic luxuries, which were in great demand in Europe. The year was 1271, and he was traveling with his father Niccolo and his uncle Maffeo. They had joined a caravan (a party of merchants traveling together for safety) and were crossing the sweltering plain of Kamadin, near the mouth of the Persian Gulf.

EXPLORER AND STORYTELLER Marco Polo (1254–1324) was one of Europe's greatest travelers. Long before European and Chinese people had any regular contact, he trekked right across Asia to the court of China's emperor, Kublai Khan. Many Venetians did not believe Marco's stories and called them "a million lies." The wealth of detail in the yarns makes many of them believable to a modern reader, although a few historians have questioned whether Marco Polo really did travel as far as he claimed.

THE TRAVELERS RODE WEARILY ONWARD. Each night, they rested in the villages that dotted the plain. Even the smallest village had a high wall of mud bricks for protection against the bandits who terrorized the region. This morning, the travelers continued their slow march. But then, Marco noticed something unusual.

A long, low cloud had appeared on the horizon. It was not like any ordinary cloud. It was a dirty brown, the color of the plain. One of the camel drivers said that a dust storm was coming, and covered his mouth and nose with a scarf. But from that moment on, the travelers sensed that something was wrong.

The cloud grew. It stretched to the left and the right as far as the eye could see. Whatever was stirring up the dust was approaching fast. Soon, they heard a low rumble like thunder. The horizon began to shimmer with reflected light. The flashes reminded Marco of sun glinting on a sword. Then all around him, he heard the word "Karaunas!" It was an insulting name for the dreaded bandits.

For an instant, the bandits were clearly visible. They were a terrifying sight, riding in a straight row that seemed to go on forever.

Then suddenly, darkness engulfed the travelers. The more superstitious people cried out, "It's magic! The bandits have transformed the day to night so that they can slaughter us unseen."

As the dust cloud blotted out the sun, sharp sabers slashed at the travelers' canvas bags. The robbers grabbed anything of value. A few of the braver souls in the party fought back, but they were quickly overwhelmed. Bandits were riding in from all sides to join the plunder.

Marco heard his father call out, "Marco! Maffeo! This way! Quickly!"

Spurring his horse, Marco rode as fast as he could. Not far behind, the bandits chased him.

Just in time, the Polos reached a town. They dashed in, and the heavy wooden gates slammed shut behind them. They had escaped, but others were not so lucky. The bandits killed the older members of the party and sold the younger ones as slaves.

The horrific bandit attack was not the only misfortune Marco suffered. Later on, he became ill and had to rest for a whole year before continuing. In all, the journey to China took nearly four years.

Finally, the Polos reached gigantic walls surrounding the grand home of Kublai Khan. Three thousand frightening guards patrolled the six gates. Inside the walls, a shady garden sheltered them from the stifling heat. Cool water flowed from sparkling fountains, and all kinds of exotic animals roamed free. At the center of the park stood two magnificent palaces. The first was built of marble and painted with colorful murals. The second was made of bamboo covered entirely in gold. This was where Marco was to meet the ruler of half the world.

When Niccolo and Maffeo saw Kublai Khan, they threw themselves at his feet, and Marco did the same. After this traditional greeting, the Great Khan welcomed them warmly.

"You must be hungry," he said, leading them to a luxurious banquet.

"This is nothing!" Maffeo told Marco as he tasted a strange dessert made of milk and ice. "The Great Khan invites 40,000 guests to his birthday party, and he wears robes of pure gold."

There were still more surprises for Marco when he traveled around China. The empire's commerce and technology were far more advanced than in Europe. China had a rapid postal service. The Chinese heated their homes with a black rock that burned. Instead of coins, they used pieces of paper for money! Eventually, though, the Polos left China and returned to Venice. They had been away 23 years and returned dressed in filthy rags. At first, their family did not recognize them and refused to believe their fantastic stories. To prove they were telling the truth, the three travelers ripped open the linings of their coats. Out tumbled a fortune in rubies, sapphires, and diamonds!

MARCO POLO'S TRAVELS

Marco's journey to China took him through the Holy Land (Israel and Syria), Turkey, Iran, Afghanistan, and India. Then he followed the Silk Road, an ancient trade route. Marco also traveled within China, but his descriptions of this country are so vague that it is not possible to know for sure what route he followed.

The Great Khan always traveled in splendor.

THE EMPEROR OF CHINA

Kublai Khan (1215–94) was the grandson of Genghis Khan, the Mongolian warrior who conquered Asia. Kublai inherited a wealthy empire. Although he could be cruel to anyone who got in his way, he also promoted literature and art. He was eager to learn about European society, which is why he welcomed the Polos.

THE FAITHFUL TRAVELER

The story so far...

After studying Islamic law, literature, and religion in his native Morocco, Ibn Battúta decided to make a pilgrimage to Mecca (now in Saudi Arabia). This religious journey to the birthplace of the prophet Muhammad was, and still is, the duty of every Muslim except the poor and sick. Ibn Battúta left Tangier for Mecca in 1325. He stopped briefly in Tripoli (now in Libya) and was married. By the time he left Egypt, he had declared an ambition "to travel through the earth."

SLEEPING UNDER THE STARS on an Egyptian rooftop, Ibn Battúta dreamed that he was flying across Asia on the back of a great bird. When he woke up, he decided to live a wandering life and vowed never to travel any road more than once.

At first, Ibn Battúta joined other pilgrims for the journey south to Mecca, where he was to take part in important religious rituals.

Ibn Battúta joined a camel caravan leaving Mecca.

WANDERING HOLY MAN Ibn Battúta (1304–1368/9), also known as Muhammad Ibn Abdullah Ibn Battúta, was born in Tangier, Morocco. In 28 years of traveling, he visited every Muslim country in Africa and Asia. He often traveled with merchant caravans. When he returned to Morocco, people listened in amazement to his stories. He dictated his adventures in a book called *Travels*. His vivid descriptions give us a glimpse of life in the Middle Ages.

Two horsemen led the attack.

A bandit's arrow hit Ibn Battúta, but to his relief, "it had not force" and scarcely injured him.

At Mecca, the line of identically dressed pilgrims in their seamless white robes stretched as far as the eye could see. Each pilgrim looked so similar to the others that if he paused for a moment, he would never find his companions in the crowd. When Ibn Battúta had completed his duties, he left Mecca and again traveled with many other pilgrims. Their journey would take them through the desert, so to avoid the scorching heat of the day, the group set out after sunset. To find their way in the dark, they carried flaming torches, passing them to one another along the line.

At first, Ibn Battúta's urge to travel led him to explore the countries of the Middle East. But within a year, he returned to Mecca to study.

Four years later, when Ibn Battúta began to travel again, he was no longer a young pilgrim but an important Muslim scholar. This time he did not just wander wherever his curiosity took him. He had heard that Sultan Muhammad Ibn Tughluq in Delhi, India, was very generous to Muslim scholars. If he could reach India and win the sultan's favor, he could live a holy life in comfort.

He left for India in 1332, on what was nearly his last journey. On India's Punjab plain, he became separated from the main party and traveled on with just 21 others. The gently rolling land offered bandits good cover. They could hide easily among the sand dunes and escape quickly along the dry riverbeds.

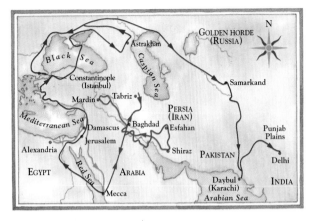

Ibn Battúta's route 1325–6
Ibn Battúta's route 1326–7

INCREDIBLE JOURNEYS
On Ibn Battúta's first journey (1325–34), he traveled across North Africa to Arabia, into Persia (Iran), north as far as the lands of the Golden Horde (now the Russian Federation), and into India. On other journeys, he visited the Maldives, Ceylon (Sri Lanka), Sumatra, China, Spain, the Sahara desert, and much of West Africa. Altogether, he traveled more than 62,000 miles (100,000 kilometers).

PILGRIMAGE TO MECCA
Mecca in Saudi Arabia is the holiest city in the Islamic world. The pilgrimage to Mecca made by Muslims is known as the *hajj*. At the center of the great mosque at Mecca is the *Kaaba*, a cube-shaped shrine. It is believed to house a sacred stone sent from heaven and is the focus of all Muslim prayer.

Sure enough, a short way into their journey a band of robbers surprised Ibn Battúta and his companions. Led by two horsemen, the 80 bandits attacked with swords, and with bows and arrows. The travelers stood their ground and fought bravely. Eventually, they beat off the raiders, killing 13 of them. When the dust settled, they tended their wounds—arrows had struck Ibn Battúta and his horse. It wasn't until midnight that the exhausted travelers limped to the safety of a nearby castle. When dawn broke, the rising sun lit up some grisly battle trophies—hanging from the castle walls were the heads of the 13 dead bandits.

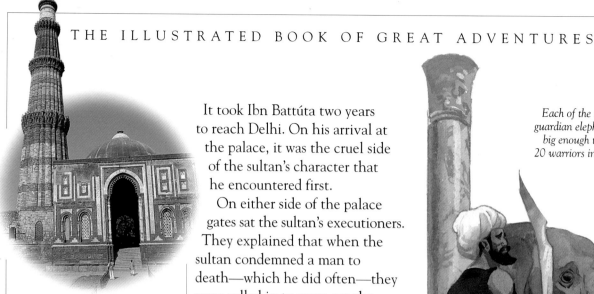

A MAGNIFICENT PALACE
The sultan's palace that Ibn Battúta visited has long since crumbled. It probably looked a lot like this entrance gate to the Qutb mosque in Delhi, India.

> *The sultan is of all men the fondest of making gifts and of shedding blood.*
>
> IBN BATTUTA

Each of the sultan's guardian elephants was big enough to carry 20 warriors into battle.

It took Ibn Battúta two years to reach Delhi. On his arrival at the palace, it was the cruel side of the sultan's character that he encountered first.

On either side of the palace gates sat the sultan's executioners. They explained that when the sultan condemned a man to death—which he did often—they were called in to carry out the sentence immediately. Then they would fling the victim's body outside the palace gates.

For the now-famous Moroccan traveler, the great gates opened. He walked past burly guards and officials in costumes adorned with peacock feathers, then stepped into the sultan's audience chamber.

A thousand pillars held up the ornately carved roof. Around the walls of the room stood 50 huge elephants. In front of the elephants stood 60 horses. In front of the horses stood an army of warriors. In front of the warriors stood a crowd of officials and servants. And in the middle of the room sat the sultan himself.

It soon became clear that the stories the traveler had heard were true. The sultan was indeed a very generous man, and Ibn Battúta was not disappointed. The sultan named him the grand *qádi* (religious leader) of Delhi and awarded him a generous pension so that he could live in luxury.

But Ibn Battúta never felt completely safe in his grand post. The sultan was fickle and moody, and his temper was legendary. Once, when he received anonymous insults, the sultan ordered his troops to clear the whole of Delhi and banish all its people.

Eventually, Ibn Battúta also fell from favor. Summoned to the palace, he found himself guarded by four of the sultan's servants. In fear of his life, Ibn Battúta turned to religion. He fasted (starved himself) and read the Koran, the Muslim holy book.

These acts of devotion impressed the sultan. He rewarded Ibn Battúta by making him an ambassador to China.

Ibn Battúta fasted and prayed to prove his devotion.

Muslims believe that the Koran is the word of God.

So, early in 1342, Ibn Battúta's travels began again. His departure from Delhi was much like his arrival eight years before. Just three days from the city, he was attacked by bandits.

Ibn Battúta fled on his horse, but it seemed that this time his luck had deserted him. His companions scattered, and when 40 bandits surrounded him, there was no escape. He flung himself to the ground and surrendered.

The sultan received his guests in the Hall of One Thousand Pillars.

Even the elephants were trained to bow to the Sultan.

The bandits robbed him and held him captive. For a few terrifying hours, Ibn Battúta believed he was going to be executed, but then one of his captors took pity on him and set him free.

Ibn Battúta had escaped death, but he was now alone in a hostile country and was forced to live as a fugitive. When, after a week, he finally found his friends, they did not recognize him. He had lost his horse and all his fine clothes. Scratches from thorns covered his arms and legs. After such a bad start, his companions begged him to change his plans and return to Delhi, but Ibn Battúta would not turn back, and he traveled on to China.

IN THE YEARS THAT FOLLOWED…

Ibn Battúta continued his travels for many more years. He was shipwrecked twice, survived an outbreak of deadly plague in Syria, and fought his way through snowstorms in the Sahara desert. By the time he died, at the age of 64, he had traveled the equivalent of three times around the world.

Ibn Battúta was engulfed in a blizzard on the High Atlas Mountains of Morocco.

COLUMBUS SAILS WEST

The story so far...

It had taken Christopher Columbus more than eight years to raise the money for his voyage of exploration, but, by 1492, he had done it. In June, he traveled to the small Spanish port of Palos to prepare his three ships, load supplies, and enlist a crew. Six weeks later, deckhands were stowing the last of the provisions.

DARING EXPLORER
Christopher Columbus (1451–1506) came from the Italian port of Genoa. He went to sea at a young age, and, by 1477, he had moved to Lisbon, Portugal, from where he sailed around the trading posts of the Mediterranean Sea and the Atlantic Ocean. In 1483, Columbus showed King John II of Portugal his plan to sail west across the Atlantic to the Indies (Asia). When King John refused to help, he approached the king and queen of Spain, who eventually paid for the trip.

"HURRY UP AND GET THOSE BALES on board the *Pinta*! The *Niña* and the *Santa Maria* are ready to sail," shouted a white-haired man with an Italian accent.

"That Admiral Columbus! He'll get us all killed," said one deckhand.

"You're right," his shipmate replied. "Sailing west to reach the East? It's a crazy idea. The Indies must be at least 1,300 leagues west. That's five times farther than any ship has ever sailed. How did Columbus trick the king and queen into paying for this crazy trip?"

"It was no trick," added a third. "Ferdinand and Isabella think there's gold to be found and that they will become rulers of any new countries Columbus discovers. Anyway, our admiral is the finest mariner in all of Spain. We won't come to any harm."

Christopher Columbus had often heard a similar argument during the the eight years it had taken him to raise the money for the trip. Now all he could think about was setting sail.

Led by Columbus in the *Santa Maria*, the little fleet of three ships set off from Spain on Friday, August 3, 1492.

The Santa Maria *had three masts and was square-rigged (had square sails).*

Columbus believed his ships would reach the Indies (Asia) in three weeks. But in case the trip took longer, he stopped at the Canary Islands and loaded enough provisions and water to last a month. On September 6th, they sailed west into the uncharted Atlantic.

Many of the mariners wept when they sailed out of sight of land. To reassure them, Columbus ordered that after 700 leagues (233 miles or 375 kilometers), they would not sail at night, in case they ran aground in the Indies.

He also used a simple trick, which he described in his logbook (ship's diary).

"To dispel their fears of a long voyage, I decided to count fewer leagues than we actually sailed. I did this so that they might not think themselves so great a distance from Spain. For myself, I will keep a secret accurate account."

They made rapid progress, but two weeks into the trip they reached the Sargasso Sea. There, floating seaweed covered the surface of the ocean. The seaweed was so thick that the ships were forced to travel very slowly. Even the experienced seamen felt afraid.

The less loyal ones plotted a mutiny (rebellion). Their plan was to throw the admiral overboard and head back to Spain.

"They have said it is insanity," Columbus wrote in his log on September 24th, "to risk their lives following the madness of a foreigner."

Fortunately, the next day, just as the sun was setting, Martin Pinzon, captain of the *Pinta*, let out a joyful cry.

"Land ahead!"

The crew members forgot their mutinous plot and climbed the rigging of their ship. Then they too swore that they could see land.

Columbus fell to his knees and thanked God.

The first man to see land could claim a reward.

After more than seven weeks at sea, the crew was afraid because it had traveled farther than anyone had ever sailed before.

NEW FOODS
Columbus discovered new foods in the New World. The countries he visited grew vegetables and fruits that were very different from those found in Europe. For example, Christopher Columbus came across corn, capsicums (peppers), and sweet potatoes. On his second trip to the New World, he brought back pineapples. These exotic foods soon became very popular in Europe.

When dawn broke the following day, the sailors' hopes were dashed. What they had thought was land was a line of storm clouds on the horizon.

Only after another two weeks did they begin to see real signs of land: A stick that had been carved with a metal tool floated in the water, and flocks of land birds appeared overhead.

Late one night, Columbus thought he saw a light in the distance. He admitted later, "I was so eager to find land that I did not trust my own senses."

But it seemed that he wasn't mistaken. At two in the morning, the *Pinta* fired a cannon, the prearranged signal that the lookouts had spotted land.

The next day, the rising sun lit up an island of exquisite beauty just 18 leagues (6 miles or 10 kilometers) away. Groves of trees grew there, and the lagoon around the island formed a natural harbor "big enough to hold all the ships in Europe."

Columbus lowered a boat from the *Santa Maria*, and seamen rowed him ashore. The captains of the *Pinta* and *Niña* followed. On the beach, they unfurled a royal banner and offered prayers of thanksgiving for their safe arrival. They named the island San Salvador and claimed it for Spain.

Almost as soon as these ceremonies were over, inquisitive native people appeared from behind the trees. Columbus described them as tall people, who all had straight legs. He also noted that not one of them had a fat stomach.

But remembering the reasons for his trip—the conquest of new lands and the discovery of treasure—Columbus did not linger. His agreement with the Spanish king and queen allowed him to keep one tenth of all the "gold, silver, pearls, gems, and other goods" that he could find.

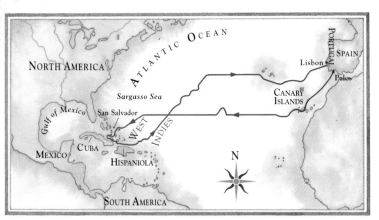

COLUMBUS'S JOURNEYS TO THE NEW WORLD
On the first of Columbus's four journeys (above) to the New World, he did not set foot on the mainland. He called the islands that he visited the West Indies because he thought that he had reached Asia (the Indies). In all, he explored Jamaica, Cuba, Haiti, and other islands, and on his third voyage, in 1498, he landed on the coast of Panama.

So the ships set off once more, this time searching for gold and treasure in Japan, which Columbus believed lay just over the horizon.

The admiral and his men never found Japan because they had reached not Asia, but the Bahamas. They visited Cuba, then traveled east, calling the next island Hispaniola (now Haiti and the Dominican Republic). The *Santa Maria* was wrecked there, and Columbus left nearly 40 men behind to establish a colony.

On October 16th, the *Pinta* and *Niña* set sail for Spain. After a month, a powerful storm struck. Gigantic waves broke over the ships, and the sailors expected to die.

Columbus was terrified that he would drown and that the world would never learn of his discoveries. So he wrote a description of the voyage on parchment, sealed it in a barrel, and tossed it into the sea.

This precaution turned out to be unnecessary. The *Pinta* and *Niña* survived the journey, and Columbus sailed home a hero.

IN THE YEARS THAT FOLLOWED…

Columbus made three more trips to the Caribbean, which he was sure was the eastern coast of Asia. The Spanish king and queen were not convinced, and Columbus was never paid the reward that he had expected for finding a westward route to the Indies and China. By 1500, many other adventurers had reached the coast of America, which became known as the New World. Christopher Columbus's brave adventure had almost been forgotten.

GOLD SOVEREIGNS

Spanish coins, called sovereigns, were stamped with the faces of the king and queen, who had paid for Columbus's expedition. He claimed the lands he found in their name but failed to find the gold they had hoped for.

VOYAGE AROUND THE CAPE

The story so far...

On July 8, 1497, Vasco da Gama set out from Portugal with four ships. He was bound for India to negotiate a trade treaty on behalf of the king of Portugal. But he was traveling past the tip of Africa (the Cape of Good Hope), a route to India that no one had ever attempted before. Four months later, the exhausted crew reached southern Africa, having sailed 4,500 miles (7,240 kilometers). The ships anchored at St. Helena Bay, 80 miles (135 kilometers) north of what is now Cape Town in South Africa.

ABOUT A WEEK AFTER ANCHORING at St. Helena Bay, Vasco da Gama went ashore to trade with the Khoikhoi, the native African people living there. He was hoping for gold, pearls, and spices. To his disappointment, they offered him only foxtail fans and shell jewelry. When he and his crew returned to the ship, one sailor stayed behind.

"I'm not finished here yet," bragged Fernão Velloso. "I want to see how these people live and what they eat. Pick me up in the rowboat later."

At first things went well. Fernão shared a feast of delicious roast seal. But when everyone had finished eating, the Africans pointed to the ship and made it clear that Fernão's visit was at an end. This wasn't what Fernão had planned at all. The boat would not return to pick him up for at least two hours. So when the Africans wandered away, Fernão followed them, ignoring their protests that he was no longer welcome.

Back on board the ship, Vasco da Gama relaxed in his chair after a sumptuous dinner.

"Splendid lobster!" he said. Then he heard a voice shouting from the shore.

Overstaying his welcome nearly cost Fernão his life.

After the rescue, the sailors quickly rowed Fernão back to the ship, which was anchored in deeper water.

When he looked out, he saw Fernão waving and calling to the ship. Behind him, a hostile crowd was gathering, and several of the men were running down the hill toward Fernão.

A few minutes later, sailors were rowing two boats frantically toward the shore. Fernão was now running along the beach with the angry Africans in hot pursuit.

A boat reached land just in time. The Africans were raising their spears and picking up rocks. Fernão dashed through the surf and dived into the rowboat headfirst.

Da Gama tossed overboard all the charts and instruments needed to plot a course at sea.

As the sailors rowed away, a hail of spears and stones flew after them, wounding Vasco da Gama in the leg and injuring three others.

The four ships were soon at sea again. But when they reached Africa's southernmost tip, they faced far greater dangers. Gale-force winds clutched at the sails and tore at the masts. For every league (3 miles or 5 kilometers) they sailed east, the wind and waves drove them two leagues westward.

As the storms raged, some of the terrified sailors on Vasco da Gama's ship talked of turning back. Da Gama called the whole crew together.

"I am as scared of drowning as you are, and I would not risk losing our ship," he reassured them. "But I have promised the king that I will sail to India. If we turn back, we must all sign a document saying why we have agreed to return." Then he took the ship's master, the pilot, and the three most experienced seamen into his cabin to sign the document.

But once the door was closed, Vasco da Gama imprisoned the five men. Then he led them before the crew with their arms and legs in chains. Taking the charts and navigational instruments from the pilot, he tossed them into the sea.

"See here!" he cried. "We do not need a navigator because God alone is our master and our pilot. From now on nobody speaks of turning back."

Vasco da Gama's bold trick frightened the crew even more than the storm and won him their loyalty. Within a few days, the weather had improved, and a favorable wind blew. They rounded the Cape and turned northward, up Africa's east coast.

OCEAN ADVENTURER
Navigator Vasco da Gama (1460–1524) was born in Sines, Portugal. He was trained in the science of sailing and became a naval officer in 1492. Da Gama made his second voyage to India in 1502 and then retired from the navy the following year. After becoming a viceroy in 1524, he again sailed to India, this time to govern the Portuguese colonies, but he died that same year.

BASIC NAVIGATION
Early explorers had few instruments to help them find their way at sea. Vasco da Gama would have had an hourglass (above) to measure short periods of time, and a simple compass with a magnetized iron needle to indicate north and south. Sailors also used the stars to figure out their position.

After dismantling their depleted supply ship, the crew set the remaining three ships on course for Calicut, the most important port in southern India. Their arrival caused a sensation. Curious crowds blocked the streets when Vasco da Gama and 13 of his officers set off to visit the Zamorin, who ruled the city. Troops fired guns into the air to clear the way to the palace, while musicians played bagpipes and drums.

The Portuguese expected a lavish reception when they arrived at the Zamorin's palace. But instead, they were kept waiting in the entrance hall. When night fell, their patience ran out; they drew daggers, overpowered the guards, and forced their way into the Zamorin's room.

A NEW ROUTE TO INDIA

Another Portuguese explorer, Bartolomeu Dias, had rounded the Cape in 1488, but Vasco da Gama was the first to take this route to India. Da Gama took advantage of strong winds and swung his ships far into the Atlantic Ocean before rounding the Cape. This route is still used by sailing ships today. Vasco da Gama sailed nearly twice as far as Columbus's expedition five years earlier.

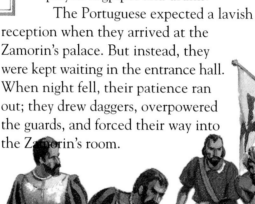

The Portuguese officers pulled out daggers and swords.

SPICES

Vasco da Gama brought back a cargo of spices. Before this, Venice was the only European source of these spices. Traders there imported them from India via Egypt and sold them at high prices. Da Gama's cargo made rare spices common. By 1504, Portuguese cooks could buy five nutmegs for the price of one nutmeg five years earlier.

There they found the Zamorin lounging on a green velvet sofa beneath a golden canopy.

He leaned on the finest, whitest cushions Vasco da Gama had ever seen, and he wore luxurious silks embroidered with gold thread. When the Zamorin smiled, Vasco da Gama noticed that his teeth were stained black from chewing betel nuts. He spat the husks into a huge, solid gold spittoon.

The Zamorin welcomed the Portuguese as brothers despite their violent entrance. But when Vasco da Gama proposed a trade treaty with Portugal, the Zamorin quickly changed the subject. Their brief visit was over, and da Gama and his officers returned in the monsoon rain to their lodgings.

The next day, they unpacked the gifts they had brought—rolls of striped cloth, hats, six washbasins, strings of coral beads, sugar, oil, and honey.

These inexpensive novelties had delighted the Khoikhoi in Africa, but they were hardly fit for the wealthy Zamorin.

"The Zamorin's spittoon was bigger than these bowls, and it was solid gold," sighed da Gama.

When the Zamorin's agents saw the gifts, they sniggered. To hide his difficulty, da Gama lied.

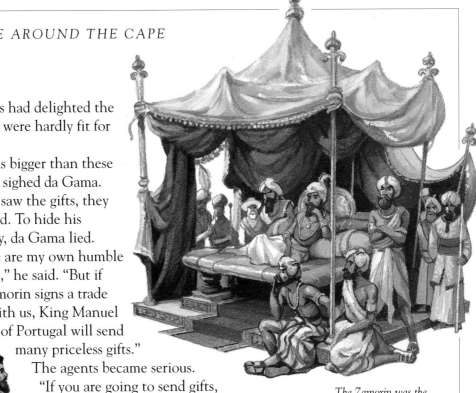

"These are my own humble presents," he said. "But if your Zamorin signs a trade treaty with us, King Manuel of Portugal will send many priceless gifts."

King Manuel of Portugal sent Vasco da Gama to negotiate with the Zamorin.

The agents became serious. "If you are going to send gifts, send only gold," they said. Without another word they turned and left. It was a disappointing end to a daring and dangerous voyage.

Vasco da Gama left India after three months. The return journey was as difficult as the outward one. Instead of storms, the ships drifted in a flat calm. The crews suffered from a strange new disease called scurvy, which later troubled all sailors who stayed at sea for months on end.

Vasco da Gama hoped to establish trading links with the local Indian merchants.

The Zamorin was the Hindu sovereign of Calicut and its surrounding area.

FRUITFUL CURE
Scurvy causes spongy gums and bleeding under the skin. It can be deadly if it is not treated. The simple cure—vitamin C from fresh fruit—was not discovered until the 18th century.

When they cruised into Lisbon harbor, Vasco da Gama and his men rejoiced, but their relief at coming home was tinged with sorrow. Scurvy had killed many of the crew, including Vasco da Gama's own brother. The pale and exhausted survivors got a heroes' welcome. A small fleet of ships accompanied them for the last few days at sea. Guns fired a salute as they dropped anchor. King Manuel himself greeted Vasco da Gama and honored him with a pension and gifts of land.

Vasco da Gama's adventurous voyage began a new era of trade and discovery for Portugal and made the nation a great world power.

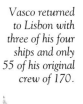

Vasco returned to Lisbon with three of his four ships and only 55 of his original crew of 170.

THE SIEGE OF TENOCHTITLAN

The story so far…

In the 25 years following Columbus's voyage, Spanish settlers colonized the largest islands in the Caribbean. By 1519, stories were spreading of the fabulous golden riches on the American continent. The governor of Cuba chose Cortés to lead an expedition of trade and exploration to the mainland. But Cortés was more ambitious. He dreamed of conquest and of returning laden with golden treasures.

THE AMBITIOUS EXPLORER
Even as a schoolboy, Hernán Cortés (1485–1547) was proud, ruthless, quarrelsome, and mischievous. He often caused trouble for his aristocratic parents. When he grew older, he became fascinated with the lands that Columbus had discovered (see pp. 20–23). When he was just 19 years old, he sailed to the West Indies. After getting a job as a minor official, his power and influence began to grow rapidly.

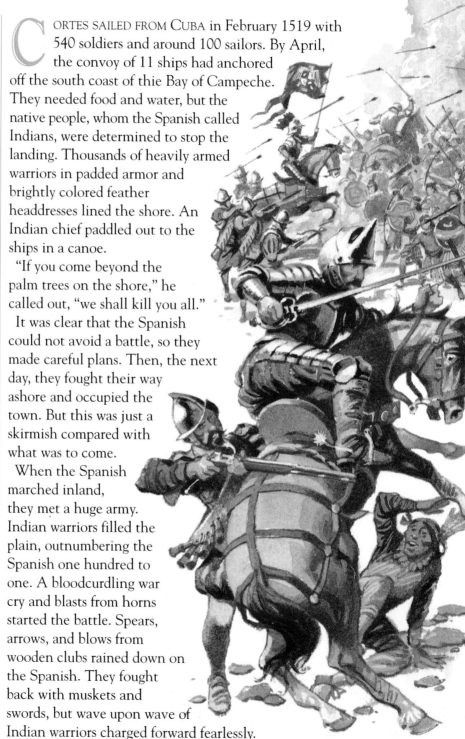

CORTES SAILED FROM CUBA in February 1519 with 540 soldiers and around 100 sailors. By April, the convoy of 11 ships had anchored off the south coast of thie Bay of Campeche. They needed food and water, but the native people, whom the Spanish called Indians, were determined to stop the landing. Thousands of heavily armed warriors in padded armor and brightly colored feather headdresses lined the shore. An Indian chief paddled out to the ships in a canoe.

"If you come beyond the palm trees on the shore," he called out, "we shall kill you all."

It was clear that the Spanish could not avoid a battle, so they made careful plans. Then, the next day, they fought their way ashore and occupied the town. But this was just a skirmish compared with what was to come.

When the Spanish marched inland, they met a huge army. Indian warriors filled the plain, outnumbering the Spanish one hundred to one. A bloodcurdling war cry and blasts from horns started the battle. Spears, arrows, and blows from wooden clubs rained down on the Spanish. They fought back with muskets and swords, but wave upon wave of Indian warriors charged forward fearlessly.

It seemed that they would slaughter the small Spanish army. But Cortés had a secret weapon. He had brought about a dozen horses, and now his cavalry rode onto the battlefield. The Indians had never seen horses before. They thought each soldier and his mount was a single fantastic beast, and they retreated in terror.

Later, the defeated Indians brought Cortés fabulous peace gifts.

"Where did you get all your gold and jewels?" Cortés asked.

"From where the sun sets," they replied. "From Mexico." Although the Spanish had not heard of Mexico, they sailed west toward the setting sun, anchored, and set up a camp among the sand dunes. News of the Spaniards' arrival spread, and before long, officials of the Aztec people who ruled the country visited the beach camp. They brought astonishing gifts—a gold sun the size of a cartwheel and a helmet full of gold dust. The officials begged the Spaniards not to travel to their capital city, Tenochtitlán. However, their magnificent gifts only made Cortés more eager. He decided to march inland to visit Montezuma, the Aztec king.

It was a dangerous plan, and some of his officers opposed it. Cortés acted swiftly and ruthlessly to stamp out rebellion. He hung two officers who were plotting to sail home and ordered that a third have his feet cut off. Then he took the boldest step of all. He ordered his sailors to sink their ships. Now there was no turning back!

The 400-mile (650-kilometer) journey to Tenochtitlán took the soldiers across three mountain ranges. At Tlaxcala, the local people, called Tlaxcaltecs, ambushed the Spanish. The soldiers drove them off with guns, but eventually, Cortés made peace with them. He discovered that they hated the Aztec lords who ruled them. So the Spanish and the Tlaxcaltecs became allies and marched onward together. Finally, after eight grueling weeks, Cortés reached Tenochtitlán. The amazing island city was set in Lake Texcoco, surrounded by smoldering volcanoes.

Montezuma himself greeted Cortés on the causeway that linked the city to the shore. The two men exchanged gifts, and then the Spaniards entered the glittering, fairy-tale city.

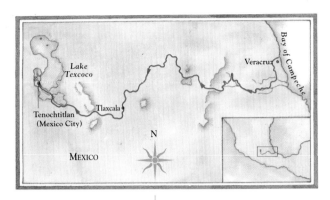

JOURNEY TO TENOCHTITLAN Cortés and his soldiers traveled halfway across central Mexico to reach the Aztec capital of Tenochtitlán. In August 1519, their march began not far from the modern city of Veracruz. Three of Cortés's captains climbed a volcano near Tenochtitlán and were the first of the explorers to see the city.

> " *I am embarking on a great and beautiful enterprise, which will be famous in times to come.* "
> **HERNAN CORTES**

By the time eight months had passed, the city had become a trap. Preparing to escape, Cortés packed some of the gold into saddlebags and luggage, yet there was still a huge pile left, enough to buy every palace in Spain. How could they bear to flee Tenochtitlán without it? But if they tried to carry any more, they would be slow, easy targets for the Aztecs, who were besieging them.

> *I shall make you, in a very short time, the richest of all men who have crossed the seas.*
> HERNAN CORTES

QUETZALCOATL MASK
Aztec craft workers created beautiful objects, not only from the gold that the Spanish were seeking, but also from materials such as feathers, clay, wood, and turquoise. Tiny pieces of brilliant blue turquoise cover the surface of this mask representing the Aztec god Quetzalcoatl. Very few gold Aztec objects survive: The Spanish melted them into ingots to make the metal easier to carry.

Cortés thought about the time that they had spent in the city. At the beginning, they had lived like kings. No, like gods! Indeed, the Aztecs had believed he was the god Quetzalcoatl.

He fingered the crucifix around his neck, consoling himself that at least they had taught the Aztecs about Christianity and ended their sun worship, cannibalism, and human sacrifices.

Cortés gazed back at the pile of gold and remembered when they had broken down the treasury wall and first seen the fabulous Aztec gold. But then, it had all gone wrong. If only Alvarado, his hot-headed captain, had not panicked and killed the Aztec leaders, Cortés might already be the king of Mexico. Instead, they were prisoners, holed up in a besieged palace like rats in a trap.

Cortés stood up and called his men together.

"I can do no more with this gold. It cannot be brought to safety. You soldiers take what you want," he told them.

The troops rushed forward and greedily stuffed the heavy gold ingots (large bars) into their clothes. Then, with their Tlaxcaltec allies, they opened the doors of the palace and crept out as silently as they could. Cortés led the way on his horse, its shoes muffled with rags.

It seemed as if the Aztec warriors, who had attacked them so bravely the previous day, had left Tenochtitlán unguarded that night. To their relief, the fugitives were free to slink through the empty squares and silent streets and set off along the causeway. In just a few minutes, they had reached the water gap where the Aztecs had removed the drawbridge.

"Bring the bridge," hissed Cortés. Spanish carpenters had built a makeshift bridge, and it spanned the gap perfectly. Cortés and his officers filed over safely. The Tlaxcaltec soldiers followed, leading horses laden with gold. Then suddenly, a shrill whistle pierced the silence. For a moment, the clouds overhead parted, and a full moon lit up the scene. To their horror, the Spaniards saw that all around them, on Lake Texcoco, were dozens of canoes filled with Aztec warriors. They had walked into an ambush!

Instantly, arrows and spears filled the air as the Aztecs attacked. Warriors clad in colorful armor made of cotton and feathers blocked the makeshift bridge. But soon the bridge was unnecessary, for the gap was filled with the bodies of dead soldiers and horses. Many of the Spanish died because of their greed. Burdened with gold, they could not fight or run, and those who fell into the water sank like stones.

Cortés and the few lucky officers who had crossed the water gap fled for their lives, fighting off their attackers with swords. They escaped and took refuge in an Aztec shrine. There they rested, and Cortés counted the cost of their humiliating retreat. He had lost some of his best soldiers, and many of the survivors were badly wounded. Most of his horses were gone; so too were all the cannons and muskets. They had even lost much of the Aztec gold.

However, Cortés was a determined man. The Aztecs had driven him from their island capital, but he was not defeated. A year later, he returned and captured the city.

FEATHER HEADDRESS
The people of Tenochtitlán valued the beautiful, bright green feathers of the quetzal bird very highly. This ornate headdress is a copy of one thought to have belonged to the Aztec king, Montezuma. Cortés sent the original to Spain, along with many other Aztec treasures.

Paddling silently in canoes, Aztec warriors mounted a surprise attack.

THE DARING ESCAPE

The story so far...

Italy was an uncomfortable place for Benvenuto Cellini in 1537. He had many enemies and often had to flee from one city-state to the next to avoid police, assassins, or the friends of people he had wounded in street fights. Powerful friends and clients protected him, but when an enemy spread false rumors about him, Cellini finally lost the support of his most important client, the Pope. He decided to pack his bags and begin a new life in France.

THE FUGITIVE
Italian goldsmith and sculptor Benvenuto Cellini (1500–71) was famous in his hometown of Florence for his great works of art – and equally for his violent temper and adventurous lifestyle. He produced magnificent jewel-encrusted masterpieces for kings and popes, but his most lasting work was the story he wrote of his own life. Despite its bragging tone, Cellini's book is as exciting and fresh as when he wrote it 450 years ago.

CELLINI WAS UNABLE TO STAY LONG IN FRANCE because he became seriously ill soon after arriving. Fearing death far from home, he decided to return to Italy in spite of possible dangers.

In Rome, his health improved, and his business as a goldsmith flourished. But within a year, Cellini's temper landed him in trouble once more. He quarreled with Girolamo, his apprentice. To get his revenge, the angry workman falsely accused Cellini of stealing the Pope's jewels during an attack on Rome 11 years earlier. Cellini's enemies used this as an excuse to have him arrested and thrown into the Castel Sant'Angelo, Rome's fortress-prison.

The injustice of his imprisonment angered and frustrated Cellini. Although he had everything that he needed to practice his trade as a goldsmith, he found it hard to work behind bars. Out of sight of his jailers, he formed a plot to escape.

He made a rope by tearing his bedsheets into long strips and braiding them together.

Breaking out of his cell, high in the castle, wasn't as easy. Using a pair of pliers that he had stolen from the castle carpenter, he pulled out the nails in the door of his cell. Cellini's skills as a sculptor helped him to hide his handiwork from the guards. With the wax that he had been given for his work as a goldsmith, he made perfect replicas of the nail heads and fixed them to the door. To the guards, they looked so much like real nails they took no notice of them. Night after night, Cellini worked away, weakening the cell door little by little. During the day, he hid the pliers and his braided rope inside his straw mattress.

Finally, he decided that the time for escape was right. He pulled the last nails from the heavy door and eased it open.

Then he crept out along the castle's silent corridors to the lavatory, which was directly under the roof. There he forced up a few of the tiles, clambered out, tied the sheet rope to a beam, and slid down it to the ground. He had escaped!

Cellini looked around. Exactly where in Rome was he? The street wasn't familiar. When he heard the snort of a sleepy horse behind him, he realized why he did not recognize his surroundings. He was not in a street at all. He had dropped into the prison stable.

Cellini was still trapped. What could he do? Pacing back and forth, he stubbed his toe painfully on a long pole lying under the straw. This gave him an idea. The pole was almost too heavy to lift, but his desperation for freedom gave him the strength of two men. Using the pole as a ladder, he climbed to the top of the wall and lowered himself down the other side onto the castle ramparts (the castle's walls and towers). Dodging patrolling guards, he tied what was left of his sheet rope to the battlements and slid down the rope till he reached the end. But his feet still didn't touch the ground. He looked up, but he was too exhausted to climb back to the ramparts. He looked down. There was nothing to see except dark shadows.

He took a deep breath and let go. The seconds seemed to pass slowly as he fell, but then his head struck the paving stones, and darkness closed in around him.

It was almost dawn when Cellini finally recovered consciousness. The fall had broken his leg, but somehow he managed to drag himself to the gates of Rome and squeeze under them into the city. At last, he was really free.

WHAT HAPPENED NEXT...
Cellini's liberty was short-lived. When the sun rose, guards at the castle saw his makeshift rope and raised the alarm. Cellini was dragged back to jail and spent many more months in his cell before he was finally freed.

Saltcellar made by Cellini

VICTIMS OF FASHION
Cellini's exotic works were soon out of fashion, and most were melted down for their gold.

CAPTURED BY PIRATES

The story so far...

Fighting raged for control of the Mediterranean during much of the 16th century. At the sea battle of Lepanto, in 1571, Christian forces from Spain and Italy defeated Muslim forces from Turkey. Spanish soldier Cervantes lost the use of his left hand in the battle but gained a written recommendation from the Austrian prince Don Juan. In 1575, Cervantes sailed for Spain, where he hoped the letter would earn him a job. Instead, it led him into trouble when pirates captured his ship.

A SOLDIER AND A WRITER Miguel de Cervantes (1547–1616), the most famous of all Spanish authors, came from a poor but noble family. Before he became a writer, he lived an exciting and dangerous life as a soldier in the Spanish infantry. At one point, he was captured by pirates and enslaved for five years. Later, he wrote of this experience in two plays and in his masterpiece novel, *Don Quixote*.

THE VICTORIOUS PIRATES stripped their Christian captives of their clothes and possessions, then herded them one-by-one aboard the Muslim galley. Eventually, it was Cervantes's turn.

"This one's worthless," grunted the scowling pirate captain. "Nobody in Algiers wants a slave with only one useful hand – he couldn't even row a galley."

Then he read the letters in Cervantes's luggage.

"This soldier is not as humble as he pretends," he exclaimed. "If Don Juan recommends him, his family will pay a golden ransom for his return."

So, mistaken for a rich man, Cervantes was taken to Algiers, where he was thrown into one of the city's three open prisons. Christian slaves were locked in these *bagnios* each night. By day, they toiled at back-breaking work around the city. The families of the wealthiest soon ransomed them (bought their freedom). But the poor and powerless were at the mercy of their masters, who often punished even minor crimes by cutting off a prisoner's nose or ears. Cervantes's injury meant he couldn't work, so he was weighed down with chains and thrown into a cell.

As time passed, the chains were removed. Free to roam the city, he tried to flee overland. When his guide deserted him, he became lost in the scorching African wilderness. Returning to Algiers, he was thrown into chains again. Only Cervantes's value as a ransom prisoner saved his life.

As soon as he could, he again made plans to flee. He arranged for his brother to send a rescue ship from Spain. It would land on a remote beach at night and carry Cervantes and 14 fellow slaves to freedom.

Until the day of the escape, the other slaves needed somewhere to hide. Luckily, Cervantes learned of a secret cave on the seacoast. A tunnel led from the cave into a garden, where undergrowth hid the cave's entrance. Before long, the 14 fugitives were concealed inside the cave.

It was several months later when the day of the escape finally arrived, and Cervantes himself joined them. Everyone was nervous. They knew dreadful punishments awaited those who were caught. They remembered the cruel fate of their fellow slave Bragadino, who was skinned alive.

It seemed an eternity until darkness fell. At last, a lookout on the beach spotted a boat. However, before he could summon the slaves, a group of local fishermen raised the alarm, shouting, "Boat! Boat! Christians!"

The lookout fled, and the sailors in the rescue boat rowed rapidly out to sea. Hidden in the cave, the prisoners knew nothing of the drama taking place outside. Another day and night passed, and still they waited for rescue.

DON QUIXOTE
In the novel that made him famous, Cervantes wrote of an old Spanish gentleman who is inspired by tales of knighthood. The gentleman changes his name to Don Quixote and rides off on his weary horse, Rozinante, to put right injustice in the world. His vivid imagination leads him to make ridiculous mistakes. For example, he fights windmills, believing they are giants.

Algerian soldiers searched for the hidden slaves.

Then, at sunrise the following day, their hopes were finally dashed. Armed soldiers burst into the cave. Cervantes rushed forward bravely and surrendered. "None of the Christians here are guilty," he cried, pleading for mercy. "I alone persuaded them to flee." But the soldiers weren't interested. They bound Cervantes's hands and feet and carried him back to the prison.

Cervantes tried twice more to escape, but he failed both times. He was finally freed when his family raised enough money to pay his ransom.

> " *I had laid a thousand schemes for my escape.* "
> DON QUIXOTE IN
> CERVANTES'S NOVEL

THE OUTRAGEOUS REBEL

The story so far...

In 17th-century London, it was not easy for unmarried women to make a living. Moll told fortunes and stole to survive. Tired of her antics and criminal habits, her so-called friends tried to get rid of her. When Moll was 23 years old, they secretly planned a new life for her, far from London. They laid a trap, getting her drunk and luring her on board a ship moored on the Thames, London's famous river.

A WILD WOMAN
Moll (Mary) Frith (1584–1659) was the daughter of a London shoemaker. As a child, she was a tomboy and a rebel. When she grew older, she dressed in men's clothes, smoked a pipe, and carried a sword. In the 17th century, London was very different from the city of today. Moll mixed with the small-time thieves, swindlers, cheats, and pickpockets who crowded the filthy streets. Eventually, she led them in a life of dangerous and illicit adventure.

WHEN SHE WOKE UP, Moll had no idea where she was. Then someone dressed as a ship's officer spoke to her. "What luggage and food have you brought on board, lass?" Immediately she guessed that she was on board a ship about to sail! She realized that she must have been sold as a laborer to someone planning to send her to America. Moll had heard false rumors that hungry American settlers – who were suffering terrible hardships – ate each other to survive. At best, she'd be almost a slave. At worst, she feared, she'd end up as a meal! Moll was furious, but there was little she could do. When she tried to escape, the crew locked her into the damp, dark, evil-smelling hold. On the decks above, she could hear the crew preparing to sail.

Time was running out! When the captain came on board, Moll pleaded for her release. She tried everything: threats, flattery, promises, and tears. Finally, his heart softened, and Moll was rowed to shore – but only after she had bribed a sailor with all the money she owned.

Betrayed by the "friends" who had put her on the boat, Moll joined a gang of thieves. To become a member, she had to take a test. Her villainous new friends first asked her a few questions, then examined her hands to make sure she hadn't been branded (burned with a hot iron to mark her as a thief).

Moll had not been branded, and the pickpockets were pleased to see that she had long fingers, perfect for dipping into rich men's pockets. Moll learned her trade well, and her skill at slicing away the coin purses that hung from people's belts quickly earned her the nickname Moll Cutpurse.

Soon, all of London had heard of Moll, and not only because she was a famous villain. She flouted the rules of London society by wearing men's clothes. This was considered outrageous in 17th-century England, and Moll was once arrested and punished for it. But for Moll, crime was exciting. So, when a friend bet her that she would not ride across the city in men's clothes, Moll not only took the ride, but announced her progress with a banner and blasts on a horn along the way.

Moll Cutpurse blew a horn to make sure everyone noticed what she was doing.

At first, the daring ride went smoothly, but when she reached the center of the city, things began to go wrong – a man recognized her.
"Moll Cutpurse on horseback!" he cried.
An angry crowd gathered quickly, shouting, "Come down, you shame among women, or we shall pull you down!"
Moll urged her horse to go faster, but the ragged mob surged forward, shouting, swearing, and tugging at her clothes. Frantically, Moll looked around for a way to escape – but she was surrounded.

However, her luck hadn't deserted her completely. Just as it seemed she would be dragged from the saddle and trampled in the mud, a wedding procession appeared. As suddenly as it had attacked Moll, the mob forgot her and turned to admire the bride.

Seizing her chance, Moll spurred her horse on. She fled north and hid out until evening. Then she finished her ride and won her bet.

THIEVES AND CUTPURSES
Even after pockets were invented, many people still carried money in purses outside their clothes. These purses made easy targets for thieves.

THE HANDSOME HIGHWAYMAN

The story so far...

Travel was dangerous in the 17th century because bands of highwaymen (armed robbers) lurked along lonely stretches of road. Duval was a highwayman with a difference. While his daring holdups quickly made him England's most wanted criminal, many women admired his stylish clothes and perfect manners. Every time Duval robbed a carriage, he took a great risk. The king offered a huge reward for Duval's capture, as much cash as most men earned in a year.

A FASHIONABLE BANDIT Claude Duval (1643–70) was born in Normandy, France. When he was 14 years old, he took a job looking after the horses of a group of English noblemen. In 1660, his employer returned to England, and Claude went with him, working as a footman. But the life of a servant did not suit him, and some time in the next six years, he found a new profession – highway robbery.

JOLTING ALONG THE RUTTED ROAD, the horse-drawn coach set off across a wide pasture. This was the most dangerous part of the journey. All three passengers shivered as they passed a gibbet. On the arms of its wooden frame, the dead bodies of executed highwaymen rotted. It was a warning to other highwaymen that they could expect no mercy if they too were caught. The well-dressed gentleman inside the coach smiled at his wife to reassure her.

"Don't worry, my dear, we shall be back in London within two hours, and we have seen no trace of highwaymen since our journey began. They won't bother us now," he said.

The words had hardly left his lips when the passengers heard a drumming of hooves on the road behind them.

"Oh my, oh my!" cried the serving maid. "I believe we are being attacked."

Her mistress saw that this was true. Five masked horsemen were galloping alongside the coach, their pistols pointed at the terrified coachman. But the woman was determined not to be frightened. To keep up her spirits, she drew a small flute

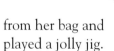

from her bag and played a jolly jig.

Within moments, the flute solo was a duet. When the leader of the robber brigade rode up to the coach door, he too was playing a flute. The three travelers stared at the highwayman. They had been expecting a vagabond splashed with the mud of the road. Instead, they saw a smartly dressed man on a thoroughbred horse.

When he spoke to the gentleman, who trembled with fear in a corner of the carriage, his voice had more than a hint of a French accent.

"Sir, your lady plays excellently, and I doubt not that she dances as well. May I have the honor of dancing with her on the meadow?"

THE HANDSOME HIGHWAYMAN

A set of gibbet chains was made especially to fit each criminal.

The serving maid's jaw dropped in amazement. "It's Duval!" she whispered. Astonished by the unexpected request, the gentleman agreed, and his wife stepped from the coach. Outside, she danced the coranto (a fashionable, lively dance) with the dapper robber. Despite his heavy riding boots, the highwayman stepped as lightly as the best London dancing master. Then he gallantly led his partner back to her seat in the coach.

However, his business was not finished. He turned again to her husband. "Sir, you have forgotten to pay for the music," he told him.

Swiftly, the gentleman replied, "No, I have not!" and pulled £100 (about $160 today) from under the seat. Duval weighed the purse in his hand.

"Sir, you are generous," he said, "so I shall excuse you the other £300." And with this, he spurred his horse and disappeared in a cloud of dust, followed by his criminal companions.

Back in the coach, the gentleman wondered how the polite highwayman could possibly have known exactly how much money he was carrying. His wife was still flushed with excitement at her dance with the daring Duval. The serving maid just fanned herself with relief at their lucky escape.

It was incidents such as this that made Claude Duval famous.

Soon others imitated his stylish clothes and gracious manners,

GIBBET CHAINS

For the 17th-century traveler, the bodies of executed highwaymen were a common sight. They hung from gibbets, wooden frames built at crossroads and at other busy places. An iron cage, called a set of gibbet chains, held the rotting body together. The chains also stopped the victims' relatives from cutting down and burying the corpses.

and Duval was blamed for every polite robbery that took place.

Then, in 1669, Duval was captured. Fashionable and aristocratic ladies visited him in prison, but none could get him released. As he was taken for execution, his admirers followed him wearing masks to hide their identities.

The highwayman wore fine clothes and spoke politely.

THE REAL ROBINSON CRUSOE

The story so far...

In 1703, Alexander Selkirk joined the crew of a privateer (a government fighting ship). By September of the following year, his ship had reached the west coast of South America. There Selkirk argued with the captain and demanded to be put ashore on the Juan Fernández islands. At the last minute, he changed his mind, but the captain would not allow the quarrelsome officer to return to the ship. Selkirk was left alone on the island.

THE CASTAWAY
Alexander Selkirk (1676–1721) was the son of a Scottish leather worker. He grew up to be a troublesome boy, and when he was 19 years old, he led a riot and then ran away to sea to avoid punishment. After his Pacific island ordeal, "Sandy" Selkirk went back to Scotland, but he later returned to sea as a British naval officer. He died off the coast of Africa when an epidemic swept through his ship.

SELKIRK WATCHED THE SHIP SAIL AWAY until its tallest mast disappeared. Only then did he turn and look at his isolated jungle home. The castaway scarcely noticed the astonishing beauty and abundant wildlife of Juan Fernández; he was overcome with loneliness.

Eventually, hunger distracted him. He loaded his musket and went in search of food. Long-gone settlers had released many of their animals, such as goats, on the island. That night, Selkirk feasted on tender kid grilled over a driftwood fire. Large leaves from a tree, which he called a cabbage tree, provided his vegetables. After eating, he drifted off to sleep.

The night's chill broke his dreams. But the cold wasn't all that had woken him. Something was pulling at his foot! Groggily, he jerked back the blanket. A huge, sleek brown rat was gnawing his shoe. He jumped to his feet, and all around him rats scampered away. Selkirk scarcely slept a wink all that night.

By dawn, he had figured out how to rid himself of the rats – and also make his loneliness more bearable. Using tasty morsels of goat meat, he tempted a few of the island's many cats into his camp. Soon a hundred guarded him as he slept. He cherished their company, singing them hymns and reading to them.

As the weeks of isolation turned to years, thorns shredded Selkirk's clothes, and his shoes fell to pieces. When his gunpowder ran out, he chased the goats and wrestled them to the ground.

Once, this method of hunting almost killed him. He had cornered a goat on a high crag. As he leaped to grab it, they both fell into the undergrowth.

But to Selkirk's horror, they kept on falling and falling. The bushes hid a ravine!

He would have died had he landed on the ground. But the goat broke his fall, losing its own life and saving Selkirk's.

When Selkirk came around, it was night. He was so dazed and bruised that another day passed before he could crawl back to his hut.

Other dangers came from the sea. Daily, he scanned the horizon for ships – and not just for rescuers. Spaniards, he believed, would murder or enslave him. He hid when Spanish ships moored in the island's bay. Once, though, Selkirk wasn't quick enough. As he dashed away, musket shots whistled past his ear. Only his fitness and agility saved him. He shinnied up a tree and sat motionless in its branches until the Spanish sailors lost interest in the chase.

After more than four years on the island, Selkirk saw the sight he'd been longing for – the mastheads of two British sailing ships.

ISLA ROBINSON CRUSOE
The island off the coast of Chile where Selkirk was marooned is now called Isla Róbinson Crusoe. This is because a few years after Selkirk's adventure, his story caught the imagination of Daniel Defoe, an English writer. Defoe added some extra details from the experiences of other castaways and wrote a novel called *Robinson Crusoe*. It was first published in 1719 and is still popular today.

> " *I am cast upon a horrible desolate island, void of all hope of recovery.* "
> ROBINSON CRUSOE
> IN DANIEL DEFOE'S NOVEL

He lit a beacon and watched with growing excitement as a rowboat headed for the shore. Then, to his horror, it turned back. Desperately, he stoked his fire. The flames rose higher than his head. But the boat disappeared into the evening darkness. How could they have missed his signal? In fact, the sailors had seen Selkirk's beacon, but they had mistaken it for a Spanish fire. When the crew finally rescued him, two days later, the "King of Juan Fernández Island" was a strange sight indeed. His long beard and goat-skin clothes made him look "as wild as the goats themselves."

BLACKBEARD THE PIRATE

The story so far...

Pirates were often welcomed in the Caribbean during the 17th century because they sold their stolen cargoes at bargain prices. However, by the start of the 18th century, pirate gangs were becoming increasingly violent, and things were getting out of control. Pirate captains, such as the frightful Blackbeard, roamed the Caribbean and the east coast of America, plundering ships and terrifying their crews.

RUISING UP THE NORTH CAROLINA COAST, the *Queen Anne's Revenge* looked much like any other merchant ship. Only when she drew closer did the sailors on a Boston-bound schooner notice the black flag flapping at the masthead. The flag had a grisly emblem—a skeleton and a red heart dripping with blood. It was a pirate ship!

The pirate captain shouted threats and curses from the deck. He was a scary-looking figure. His jet-black hair cascaded over the shoulders of his crimson coat. The leather straps across his chest held six pistols, and tucked into his belt were two cutlasses. But it was his beard that made the captain impossible to forget. It was so huge that it almost covered his face, and tied into it were smoking fuses that made him look like the devil himself.

"It's Blackbeard!" shouted the mate of the schooner. "If we want to live to see another day, we'd better surrender now."

Blackbeard climbed from the hold looking horrifyingly evil.

BLACKBEARD THE LEGEND
Edward Teach (d. 1718) from Bristol, England, was one of the most famous pirates of the 18th century. Under the nickname Blackbeard, he terrorized everyone he met, including his own crew. His legendary reputation was built up after only two years raiding ships in the Caribbean and off America's eastern shore.

Blackbeard's ship was intended to scare anyone who saw it. The *Queen Anne's Revenge* was bigger than any other pirate ship of the time, and Blackbeard had added extra cannons after capturing it in 1717.

It wasn't just his victims that feared him. Blackbeard's own crew told stories of his wild drinking and fierce temper. One day, he dared his crew, "Let us make a hell of our own and see how long we can bear it."

Two crew members took up the challenge and followed him into the hold. There, he lit a fire and threw on sulphur, producing a choking, poisonous smoke. Only when the two men, gasping and coughing, begged for air would Blackbeard open the hatches.

He climbed out last, delighted he could endure the choking fumes longer than anyone else.

Feats like these made Blackbeard famous. So in the spring of 1717, when his ship sailed up the Ashley River to Charleston, South Carolina, the town's inhabitants feared the worst. Blackbeard and his band of 300 pirates spent a week stopping ships, stealing their cargoes, and capturing their crews. They even imprisoned a town councilmember and his four-year-old son.

Then the pirate captain demanded a ransom—a medicine chest to treat his crew. He swore that unless the townspeople sent the chest, he would kill his 80 hostages and send their heads to the governor of South Carolina.

One of the hostages rowed ashore with several of Blackbeard's men to deliver the demand to the remaining town councilmembers. The pirates swaggered around the streets, drinking and enjoying their holiday on shore.

A few days later, Blackbeard's fleet returned to Charleston harbor to collect the ransom. Everyone believed the pirates were about to attack. Men gathered weapons, and children ran through the streets to hide.

But to the enormous relief of the townspeople, the ransom was delivered before the deadline Blackbeard had set. Blackbeard freed his captives and sailed north to continue plundering ships.

Soon he thought up a daring new scheme, but his plans did not include all his crew. The favored few joined Blackbeard on a new, smaller ship.

Blackbeard's men were a vicious, brutal gang.

The town of Charleston, South Carolina, lies on the Ashley River, which has many inlets and islands. It became part of the United States in 1788, 70 years after Blackbeard terrorized the region.

BLACKBEARD'S FLAG
Not every pirate flag was a Jolly Roger (skull and crossbones). Many pirate captains flew a plain black or red flag or had their own "trademark" pennant. On Blackbeard's flag, a skeleton drank a toast to death and a bleeding heart warned of the dangers of resisting attack.

Abandoning a sailor on a deserted island was called marooning. It was a favorite pirate punishment.

The unlucky crew members were marooned on a small island without food or water.

Blackbeard's new plan began with a crooked treaty. The governor of North Carolina agreed to ignore Blackbeard's piracy in exchange for a share of his loot. Blackbeard no longer needed to fear capture. He could raid any ship he chose and take whatever he wanted.

But the honest merchants and planters were sick of Blackbeard's gang. They called on the navy to capture the pirate—dead or alive. So, one morning in 1718, two naval sloops (ships) sailed out of the mist towards Blackbeard's ship anchored off the North Carolina coast. Blackbeard had spies everywhere and was expecting an attack. He fired a warning shot, then he raised a glass of rum to the men who had come to capture him.

"Damn you, you villains!" he shouted. "Who are you, and where do you come from?"

"You may see we are no pirates," called back Lieutenant Maynard, the commander of one of the naval sloops.

The lieutenant told his men to row the ship closer. But they were easy targets on the open deck. Gunfire from the pirate ship killed and injured nearly 30 men, and Maynard sent the rest to hide below.

When the ships drifted closer together, there were only a couple of sailors to be seen on the deck of the navy vessel. Blackbeard was surprised at his good luck.

"Let's jump on board and cut them to pieces," he shouted.

The pirates tossed a couple of grenades on the deck and swarmed aboard.

"All hands on deck!" cried Maynard.

His valiant seamen rushed out, and a savage battle began. As the smoke cleared, Maynard came face to face with Blackbeard himself. Both men fired their pistols. Rum had ruined Blackbeard's aim; only Maynard's bullet hit its target. But Blackbeard hardly flinched. He drew his gleaming cutlass. Maynard lifted his sword to defend himself, but with a crushing blow Blackbeard snapped the blade in two. Suddenly defenseless, Maynard fumbled for a pistol. He was too slow! Blackbeard was upon him, his sword raised above his head. But before the pirate could strike the fatal blow, one of Maynard's men cut Blackbeard's throat. Maynard saw his chance. He cocked and fired his pistol, and the pirate chief dropped to the deck—dead.

When Maynard's ship returned to the harbor, it had a grisly new figurehead—hanging from the bowsprit was Blackbeard's head.

Stranded pirates had to beg for help from passing ships.

Aloe vera

Lavender

Pearls

Thistle

18TH-CENTURY MEDICINES
The medicine chest that Blackbeard demanded probably did little to heal his crew's ills. Medical treatment in the 18th century was quite primitive, mixing traditional herbal cures with superstition and astrology. The chest would have contained treatments that we think of as herbs or spices today, such as chamomile or nutmeg, along with more exotic potions, such as a solution made of human skull.

BLACKBEARD THE PIRATE

In the early 1700s, sailors did not wear uniforms; instead they wore "short clothes," which were suitable for climbing on rigging.

OCRACOKE INLET
The British navy caught up with Blackbeard in the network of rivers and small islands around North Carolina (the British then ruled much of North America's east coast). Blackbeard's ship was anchored in a bay called Ocracoke Inlet.

CUTLASS
Blackbeard fought with a cutlass, a short sword. According to legend, buccaneers (17th-century Caribbean pirates) invented the cutlass, but it's more likely that pirates simply used whatever weapons they could get their hands on. A short sword, like a cutlass, made a useful weapon at sea because a longer blade caught on the ropes that hung around the deck.

Flintlock pistols fired only one shot before needing to be reloaded. After firing a shot, pirates often used them as clubs.

CAPTAIN COOK'S LAST JOURNEY

The story so far...

Cook's second triumphant trip to the Pacific made him the greatest explorer of his time. He retired from the navy with a generous pension but, in 1776, was tempted back to sea. This time, his mission was to find a northern way out of the Pacific: either west, around Siberia, or east, around Alaska. His ships, *Discovery* and *Resolution*, would sail from England to the North Pacific via South Africa, Tasmania, and New Zealand.

CAPTAIN COOK
English explorer James Cook (1728–1779) learned to sail on a ship transporting coal. After joining the navy, his personality and abilities earned him rapid promotion. In 1768, as commander of a scientific expedition to the Pacific, he made the first maps of New Zealand's coast. This voyage also made him famous for his success in protecting his crew from deadly scurvy (see p. 27). Between 1772 and 1775, he explored more of the Pacific, making many sensational discoveries and returning with new sea maps.

COOK'S SHIP *RESOLUTION* SET OFF with an unusual and noisy cargo. England's king was sending gifts of cattle, pigs, sheep, and goats to the Pacific Island chiefs. Cook himself added rabbits and horses when they stopped at a South African port. He remarked that *Resolution* was almost an ark!

By the following April, they had reached the Friendly Islands (now known as Tonga). Cook had given the islands this English name after the warm reception that he had received there four years earlier. This time, the local people were as welcoming as he had remembered them. Cook and his crew lingered on the beautiful tropical islands for nearly three months.

Then their voyage took them on to Tahiti and north into uncharted oceans. In January, the mountain peaks of Hawaii appeared on the horizon; Cook's crewmen were the first Europeans to see them.

When Cook landed, the islanders greeted him as though he were a returning god and threw themselves at his feet. The expedition stayed in Hawaii for two weeks before continuing north once more.

By April, the ships had left the balmy South Seas far behind. They were ploughing through icy waters off the coast of Alaska, when *Resolution* sailed into a thick fog that muffled sound and hid everything from view. Normally, Cook would have anchored the ship and waited for clear weather. But they were in deep water and the wind was gentle, so he pressed on. For safety, he sent a sailor, or leadsman, to take soundings (measure the water's depth).

The leadsman threw the end of his lead line (weighted rope) into the sea. "Deep 17, 17 fathoms deep!" His voice rang through the eerie silence.

The lead line had sunk to the level of a red marker that told him the sea bottom lay 17 fathoms (102 feet or 33 meters) below.

"By the mark 9, 9 fathoms deep!" he sang out just moments later.

The people of the Pacific Islands had few possessions, and those they did have, they shared. But Cook called them thieves when they tried to share his possessions or those of his crew. He punished "criminals" severely. Once he cut off the ear of a man who stole his sextant (a navigating tool).

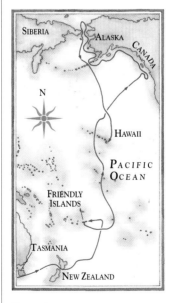

The water under the ship was fast becoming shallower. There was another splash as he threw the line again.

"By the mark 3, 3 fathoms!" he called as the line ran out to the three leather tags marking 3 fathoms (18 feet or 5.5 meters).

The leadsman's last shout echoed loudly on both sides of the ship. Hidden in fog were cliffs to the left and right! Suddenly, there was another warning sound—surf breaking on rocks. They were just moments from shipwreck.

"Let go anchor!" shouted Captain Cook.

Scarcely any of the heavy cable ran out before the anchor struck the sea bottom. The sailors braced themselves. They waited for the sickening crash of *Resolution* hitting the rocks. Miraculously, it never came.

When the mist cleared, the crew stared in disbelief. They had sailed blindly through a shallow channel between two jagged towers of rock. By sheer good luck, *Resolution* had passed through a central passage of water scarcely wider than her own hull.

Cook gaped in horror. He took off his hat and wig, and wiped his brow.

"Good grief!" he gasped. "I wouldn't have tried that on a clear day!"

COOK'S FINAL JOURNEY
After this narrow escape, Cook's luck ran out. He couldn't find a northern way out of the Pacific, so he turned for home. But in Hawaii, one of his men got into an argument over a stolen boat and shot an island chief. Angry Hawaiians retaliated by killing Captain Cook himself.

DANGEROUS TIMES IN WILD LANDS

WITH THE START OF THE 19TH CENTURY,
a new chapter began in the story of adventure.
In earlier times, intrepid mariners had charted
the coasts of distant continents. Now a new
generation of pioneers, colonists, and travelers
would explore and settle the wild
interiors of those continents.
In huge expeditions, they explored America's
raging rivers and Australia's desert center.
As lone travelers, they trekked to the
mysterious cities and swamps of Africa.
These new adventurers often carried guns to
defend themselves against unknown dangers.
But some also went equipped with scientific
instruments. The thrill of discovery was no
longer enough. In a new age of scientific
curiosity, everything novel and surprising had to
be collected, labeled, measured, and counted.

*Some of the 19th century's most adventurous
characters were rebels and outlaws. Australian
outlaw Ned Kelly was a bank robber and
a murderer, but his final battle made him a
popular hero in "Ned Kelly's Last Stand."*

EXPLORING SOUTH AMERICA

The story so far...

Alexander von Humboldt's long-planned scientific expedition finally began when he received permission to explore the Spanish colonies of South America. For his assistant and companion, he chose Aimé Bonpland, a young French physician and botanist. The two intrepid travelers set out from the Venezuelan city of Caracas in March 1800. They were aware that many dangers lay ahead. But nothing quite prepared them for the ordeals that they would face in the Amazon rain forest.

JUNGLE EXPLORER
German scientist and explorer Alexander von Humboldt (1769–1859) first became interested in botany (the study of plants) while at college in Berlin. He also mastered geology and, later, took a job as an inspector of mines. As he trudged along dark, dripping tunnels, he dreamed of exploring hot tropical jungles. When his mother died, he inherited the money to make his dream a reality.

THE LUXURIANT SOUTH AMERICAN PLANTS AND BEASTS astonished and delighted the pair.

"How brilliant the plumage of the birds and the colors of the fishes," Humboldt wrote. "Even the crabs are sky blue and gold!"

But the rain forest also terrified and tormented Humboldt and Bonpland. By day, they braved cannibals and enormous boa constrictors. By night, they heard hungry jaguars roaring in the darkness. On the forest floor, they saw strange insects scurrying in every direction. In the air, humming clouds of bloodthirsty mosquitoes blocked the sun. Their bites made Humboldt's hands so swollen that he could hardly hold a pen. He tried everything to escape the mosquitoes—he stood in waterfalls and even wrote his journals in huts filled with choking smoke. But insects did not just bite the travelers—they ate their food too. When their supplies were gone, hunger and thirst forced the two men to eat ants and to drink the brown waters of the Orinoco River. Roast monkey was a rare luxury.

Enduring the hardships of the jungle would have been slightly easier if the moist heat hadn't rotted their plant specimens. Tropical storms made their discomfort worse and, at the beginning of April, nearly killed them.

They were traveling down the majestic Orinoco when a storm gathered. The approaching clouds made Humboldt uneasy.

Flesh-eating piranhas swam in the muddy Orinoco.

He gazed at the riverbanks and noticed that floating lazily in the shallows were huge crocodiles. Moments later, rain blocked his view. The deluge was so heavy that it was hard to believe a cloud could hold so much water. Soon pools were forming in the bottom of the boat. Humboldt wondered whether he would be able to swim to shore. He looked at the instruments and supplies in his canoe. If he lost them, it would be impossible to continue his scientific studies. He looked back at his botanist companion. Although Bonpland was bailing frantically, the water level in the canoe kept rising. Waves were beginning to lap over the sides.

Suddenly, Humboldt heard several loud splashes. He turned to see his guides swimming for shore. This made the boat float higher in the water, but without their guides' expertise, the Europeans were helpless. If they escaped drowning and dodged the crocodiles' jaws, their chances of surviving alone in the jungle were slim. Rescue was unlikely— even Indian canoes were rare on that part of the river. The two men grimly discussed what to do.

"Climb on my back, Herr von Humboldt," suggested Bonpland courageously, "and I will swim for the shore."

But Humboldt never had to put his friend's strength to the test. The storm ended as suddenly as it had begun. A gentle breeze blew the canoe to the bank, where their guides rejoined them.

ART FOR SCIENCE
There were no cameras in 1800. One of the ways explorers recorded their findings was to paint or sketch them. This painting of a plant (*Melastoma coccinea*) is one of more than 3,000 completed by Bonpland.

Bonpland's frantic bailing could not stop water from filling the canoe.

THE HUMBOLDT MONKEY
Some of the plants and animals discovered by Humboldt were named after him. One of them, this woolly monkey (*Lagothrix lagothricha*), was later in danger of extinction. Humboldt was among the first to recognize that all life forms depend on each other, and he would be pleased to know that the monkey's risk of extinction is now low.

Humboldt's route 1800

HUMBOLDT'S DISCOVERIES
On their first journey, the explorers joined the Orinoco some way from the river mouth. They traced its course upstream, then carried their boat overland to the Amazon. By following the Casiquiare Waterway from the Amazon to the Orinoco, they proved that the two huge rivers connect.

In July 1800, Humboldt and Bonpland returned to the coast of Venezuela. A line of 14 mules carried their instruments and the 12,000 specimens that they had collected. But for Humboldt, exploration was addictive.

He and Bonpland soon began another journey, this time to Cuba and on to Ecuador. Volcanoes fascinated Humboldt, and in the Andes mountains that divide Ecuador, there were plenty to investigate. He hoped to climb Chimborazo, the tallest volcano in the country, but was disappointed to reach "only" 19,280 feet (5,880 meters). Nevertheless, this ascent set a world altitude record that was unbeaten for 30 years.

He had more luck with Pichincha, which towers above Quito, Ecuador's capital city. He left his heaviest instruments behind and climbed with two local guides. Their first attempt failed because Humboldt suffered from dizziness, breathlessness, and confusion—the symptoms of mild mountain sickness. At its worst, mountain sickness causes nosebleeds, headaches, and unconsciousness. Humboldt was the first to recognize its cause—lack of oxygen. Without the oxygen tanks that modern mountaineers carry, Humboldt's climbs were especially dangerous.

Before beginning their second attempt, the three men sat disheartened beneath the mountain. They stared up at its towering walls of volcanic rock. Humboldt remembered a similar volcano he had climbed on the Atlantic island of Tenerife. There he had scrambled to the top of a rocky ridge on his hands and knees.

So they set off in the same way up Pichincha, at first finding their footing cautiously on the snow that covered much of the volcano. The snow seemed solid enough, and although they had no ropes, ice axes, or other safety equipment, they were soon climbing with confidence. Suddenly, Aldas, one of the guides, cried out in terror as the snow gave way underneath him.

"Help me!" he yelled. "There's nothing under my feet."

He had fallen into a deep crevasse and was terrified that the volcano might swallow him at any moment. Humboldt and the other guide rushed to pull him to safety. Fortunately, Aldas had landed on a ridge of compacted snow a few yards down the deep crevasse.

The three men were alarmed by the fall. At first, both guides refused to go any higher, and Humboldt decided to continue alone. However, when Aldas saw him scrambling safely onward, he followed, and the pair gingerly picked their way up.

They climbed without maps and with no clear idea of the best route to the top. The steeply sloping, narrow paths gradually became broader and more level as they climbed higher and higher into the swirling clouds.

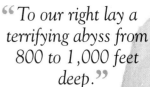

"To our right lay a terrifying abyss from 800 to 1,000 feet deep."

HUMBOLDT

Slowly they began to notice signs that they were approaching the crater. The stench of sulfur prickled their nostrils, the ground beneath their feet had grown warmer, and the snow had melted in places.

They were walking on one of the few remaining patches of snow when a rock loomed out of the dense mist. Humboldt was in front, and as he approached, he noticed something alarming. Between the snow on which he was standing and the base of the rock, only a few paces ahead, he could see flickering bright red flames.

Instantly, he realized that they were walking on a fragile ice bridge spanning the volcano's fiery crater. He leaped onto a rocky ledge, turned around, and grabbed Aldas by the poncho, pulling him onto safe ground. A few more steps would have sent them both tumbling to certain death. They crouched on the ledge and peered into the crater. Gradually, fear turned into exhilaration and pride in their achievement.

Humboldt measured the air pressure and judged that they had reached nearly 16,000 feet (4,880 meters). Then they turned to begin their descent—but not before Humboldt had dried his boots in the heat rising from the volcanic cone!

IN THE YEARS THAT FOLLOWED…

Humboldt collected so much material on his trip that it took him nearly 25 years to organize his findings. He published them in a collection of 30 books. But he still longed to travel. At 59, he went to central Asia, a region largely unknown to Europeans.

A GRIZZLY ATTACK

The story so far...

In May 1804, Meriwether Lewis, William Clark, and 43 other men left St. Louis, Missouri. Traveling up the Missouri River in a flat-bottomed boat and two canoes, they planned to explore Louisiana. The US had bought this vast area of land, west of the Mississippi River, from France only one year before. The men would then head farther west, into unknown territory, only returning after they had reached the Pacific Ocean.

Meriwether Lewis   William Clark

LEWIS AND CLARK
Meriwether Lewis (1774–1809) was US President Thomas Jefferson's private secretary. Before that, he had been a respected army captain. William Clark (1770–1838) had once commanded Lewis in the army, and the two men were friends. President Jefferson chose the pair to lead an expedition in search of a new route to America's Pacific coast.

The expedition almost came to an end as soon as it had started. At a spot called the Devil's Raceground, strong currents drove the large boat onto sandbanks. For a terrible moment, it seemed as through the craft would overturn, pitching all the supplies into the swollen Missouri River. Everyone on board jumped into the water and pulled on the heavy boat. Somehow they managed to hold on until the current swept the boat into deeper water. The strongest swimmers then towed it to the shore.

Farther upstream, the expedition faced more hazards. Native people of the Sioux tribe were determined to block the expedition's progress. Bribes of tobacco and whisky failed to budge them, so Clark gave the people more gifts. But when Sioux warriors surrounded him, he drew his sword, and an angry argument began. However, Clark spoke no Sioux, and they spoke no English. A boatload of armed soldiers came to Clark's aid, and the argument ended quickly. After four tense days of negotiations, the Sioux finally let the expedition pass.

Other native peoples were more cooperative. The peaceful Mandan tribe allowed the expedition to build cabins for the winter near their village.

By December, it was so cold that the river froze over. The weather did not worry the hardy Mandan, who even played lacrosse naked on the ice. But several expedition members became ill, and one had to have his frostbitten toes cut off. The freezing weather lasted until February; then ice on the river further delayed the expedition until early April.

Even after the thaw, the Missouri was too narrow for their largest boat, so some of the men sailed it back to St. Louis. The remaining 32 set off into unknown territory, paddling the two canoes that they had brought with them and six more that they had made during winter.

Food had been scarce, but with the coming of spring, there was abundant game. Hunting along the riverbank one day, Lewis came across a vast herd of buffalo.

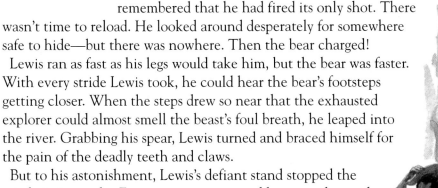

He took careful aim with his rifle and squeezed the trigger. As he watched the buffalo fall, he had the sensation that he was being watched. Just in time, he turned around to see a huge grizzly bear approaching.

Instinctively, Lewis raised his rifle—but almost immediately, he remembered that he had fired its only shot. There wasn't time to reload. He looked around desperately for somewhere safe to hide—but there was nowhere. Then the bear charged!

Lewis ran as fast as his legs would take him, but the bear was faster. With every stride Lewis took, he could hear the bear's footsteps getting closer. When the steps drew so near that the exhausted explorer could almost smell the beast's foul breath, he leaped into the river. Grabbing his spear, Lewis turned and braced himself for the pain of the deadly teeth and claws.

But to his astonishment, Lewis's defiant stand stopped the grizzly in its tracks. For a moment, man and bear gazed at each other. Then the bear wheeled around and fled. Shaking with fear and relief, Lewis resolved always to keep his gun loaded in the future.

WHAT HAPPENED NEXT...

Dodging rattlesnakes and more bears, the expedition crossed the Rocky Mountains and reached the Pacific on November 15, 1805. By the time they returned to St. Louis ten months later, the men had traveled nearly 8,000 miles (13,000 km).

SOME MUCH-NEEDED HELP
Sacajawea (shown above), a woman from the Shoshone tribe, joined the expedition at its winter camp. She became a guide and interpreter, helping the explorers negotiate with the tribes that they encountered.

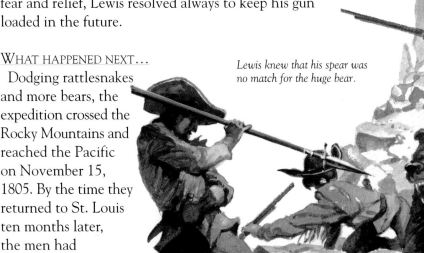

Lewis knew that his spear was no match for the huge bear.

THE WILD RIVER CROSSING

The story so far…

The year 1822 had been a good one for Davy Crockett. He had moved to a new remote frontier homestead, planted his corn, and reaped a good harvest. He had shot eight bears and plenty of other game in the autumn and early winter. But by Christmas, Davy had a problem. There was no meat left in the pantry, and he could not go hunting because he had used up his supply of gunpowder.

FRONTIER FIGHTER
Davy Crockett (1786–1836) grew up on the American frontier. Although he had only 100 days of schooling, he was smart and resourceful. He built a reputation as a leader and a fearless scout fighting Native Americans during the Creek War (1813–14). In 1821, Davy became a politician. His speeches, filled with amusing tales of backwoods life, made him a legend. Davy Crockett died fighting for Texan independence from Mexico at the battle of the Alamo.

DAVY WAS PREPARED. Although he had run out of gunpowder, he knew that his brother-in-law had another keg of powder stored for him. All Davy needed to do was fetch it.

To do this, however, he would have to cross a river swollen by the winter rains. His wife begged him not to go.

"We might as well starve as have you freeze to death or drown," she told him. But Davy was intent on fetching his powder. He packed a set of dry clothes and set off with his gun.

Davy's soft, leather moccasins crunched in the deep snow. When he reached the flooded bank, the river looked like an ocean stretched out in front of him. But he had crossed this river many times before and was determined not to be put off by the raging waters.

He stepped in. The water was so cold that, for a few seconds, it took his breath away.

Bracing himself, Davy held his bundle of dry clothes and his gun out of the water and waded in.

Anxious to be out of the freezing water as soon as possible, he splashed quickly to the edge of a deep channel. Here, the water moved much faster, and the powerful current soon swept away any debris that fell in its path. At first, Davy could see no way to cross it. Then he recognized a small tree growing from what was usually an island. The top of the tree now sprouted from foaming rapids. A fork in the tree gave Davy an idea.

He took out his tomahawk (ax), and in minutes, he had cut down a sapling and wedged its end into the fork of the tree. Wrapping his legs around the sapling, he hauled himself across.

Davy shivered in the shallow water covering the island. He knew that another fallen tree usually bridged the river here, but he couldn't see it. Waist-deep in water, he probed with a stick for several minutes until he found it. Feeling his way with his feet, he inched along the submerged log to its end.

Only a short stretch of foaming water stood between him and dry land. He knew that if he fell in, he would be lucky to survive in the icy water for more than a few minutes.

A POPULAR HERO
To aid his political career, Davy Crockett wrote his life story. First published in 1834, it became very popular. Other writers soon copied the easy-to-read, jokey style.
In the 20th century, the book appeared as a comic strip. A fictional Davy, only loosely based on the real man, featured in a TV series, and even costarred with Donald Duck.

By amazing good luck, the floodwater had carried down a log and wedged it across the final channel. Clenching his jaw to stop his teeth from chattering, Davy clambered onto the log. It rocked. He stretched out his arms to balance. Step by step, he made his way gingerly along. The trunk creaked. Davy nearly lost his balance. The log sank a little, but he was almost there.

Then suddenly, just a stride or two from dry land, the unsteady bridge spun beneath his feet. With a loud splash, Davy fell into the icy stream. He went in up to his head, but somehow managed to stand upright and keep his gun and pack above the water.

Gasping for breath, he waded the last few icy yards. On the bank, his fingers were so stiff that he could scarcely change into his dry clothes. It was some time before he could gather the strength to go on. The 5-mile (8-kilometer) trek through the snow to his brother-in-law's cabin was among the worst that he had endured.

"I didn't know," he wrote later, "how much anybody could suffer and not die."

TO TIMBUKTU IN DISGUISE

The story so far...

The route to Timbuktu was dangerous. Not only would René Caillié have to brave wild animals and harsh weather, but the people in the region were hostile to Europeans. Caillié could not afford a large expedition with armed soldiers, so he disguised himself as a Muslim, studied the Koran (the Islamic holy book), and learned Arabic. By 1827, he was ready. With Africans as his traveling companions, he set off from Sierra Leone.

DREAMS OF TIMBUKTU
As a boy, René Caillié (1799–1838) read *Robinson Crusoe* (see pp. 40–41) and longed to travel far from his home in Mauzé, a quiet French village. He dreamed of exploring Africa and of visiting the mysterious desert city of Timbuktu. No European had ever returned alive from this legendary ancient center of trade and learning. René Caillié, a baker's son, vowed that he would be the first. By the age of 20, he had visited Africa twice but was no closer to his goal. He returned to Africa in 1824, determined to succeed.

RENE CAILLIE'S TREK INTO THE AFRICAN INTERIOR was hot, tiring, and treacherous. He risked robbers, suffered raging fevers and stomach cramps, and his feet blistered. Other hazards were even more alarming. Ferocious monkeys threatened him at a water hole, and he was nearly swept away when he forded a flooded river.

Caillié put up with these hardships without complaint because he faced an even greater danger: discovery. To the Muslims of North Africa, Christians such as Caillié were evil and deserved no mercy. If the Frenchman's disguise slipped, he risked slavery or death. In Kankan, the hometown of his guide, Lamfia, he faced his hardest test. The arrival there of a pale-skinned traveler caused a minor sensation. On his first evening, Caillié's many visitors included a suspicious Arab from north of the Sahara Desert. The next day, Caillié was summoned by the town chief.

As he walked to the hut with Lamfia, Caillié felt uneasy. His anxiety turned to fear when he stepped inside. All the town's elders had gathered to question him. First, though, there was a prayer. It was a routine that he had practiced many times, but Caillié was extremely nervous. The slightest mistake could arouse suspicion. Then he might vanish forever—like other Europeans who had gone in search of Timbuktu.

Fortunately, he passed this test, but then the questions began. Lamfia told them Caillié's invented life story.

"When he was young, French soldiers invaded Egypt capturing 'Slave of God,'" Lamfia began, using the Islamic name Caillié had chosen for himself. "Christians raised him in Europe. Released in Senegal, he was free to be a Muslim again. Now he is making a pilgrimage to the sacred city of Mecca."

The town elders listened carefully and asked many questions. Caillié replied to most of them with well-rehearsed answers, but there was one question for which he was not prepared.

"What are the names of your parents, and are they still alive?" translated Lamfia.

Caillié was terrified that the town elders would guess the truth.

Caillié hesitated. His throat went dry. His palms began to sweat. If he invented names, they would want to know where his parents lived. How could he describe a place that he had never seen?

"I, I don't remember," he stammered. "I was just a boy when the Christian infidels snatched me away."

The elders talked among themselves; then they spoke to Lamfia, who translated their judgment to Caillié. His bluff had worked! The elders believed he was a genuine pilgrim. They would do everything they could to help him on his way.

Caillié needed all the help he could get. For when he set off again, a blister on his foot became seriously infected. He was forced to rest for five months while it healed. When a famine struck the village where he was recovering, he almost died of starvation.

But by March 1828, Caillié had regained his strength. He traded his umbrella for a boat ride on the mighty Niger River, and almost exactly a year after setting off, he glimpsed Timbuktu in the distance. At last, he had reached the fabulous city that he had dreamed of for many years. He wondered what secrets were hidden behind its sun-scorched, dusty walls.

THE NIGER RIVER
For the last part of his journey to Timbuktu, Caillié sailed on the mighty Niger River. He traveled in a huge pirogue (a giant open canoe). The course of the Niger had long puzzled Europeans. Exploration 20 years before Caillié's journey had added to the mystery of the region by showing that the Niger seemed to flow away from the sea! (It actually flows inland before reaching the sea at the coast of Nigeria.)

> " *On entering this mysterious city, I experienced an indescribable satisfaction.* "
> RENE CAILLIE

TIMBUKTU

The city of Timbuktu (now in Mali) lies on the southern edge of the Sahara Desert. Its position on a caravan route allowed its people to grow very wealthy by controlling trade in gold and salt. By the 15th century, it was a center of learning in the Islamic world and had a famous university. Europeans knew of the city through the stories of Ibn Battúta (see pp. 16–19) and other Arab travelers. They embroidered these factual accounts with fantastic legends. The city's reputation, its wealthy past, and its remote location made it the most desirable target for white explorers of Africa.

After spending a few days in Timbuktu, Caillié's excitement turned to bitter disappointment. Before he reached it, Caillié had guessed that the city was no longer quite as rich or magnificent as the legends and travelers' tales suggested. But he still wasn't prepared for the dust, poverty, and heat of the town. He wrote in his journal that he "had formed a totally different idea of the grandeur and wealth of Timbuktu," and he described it as "a mass of ill-looking houses built of earth." In place of the gold and fabulous riches that he had hoped for, white sand from the surrounding Sahara Desert drifted through the city's streets.

Caillié explored more of Timbuktu. He visited its king and secretly surveyed its streets and sketched its mosques. After two weeks, he'd had enough. He paid to join a caravan heading north across the Sahara.

It was a journey that he was dreading, and it began as it would continue—badly. Caillié took so long saying his farewells that the caravan of 600 camels started without him. He had to run nearly a mile (more than a kilometer) through the desert to avoid being left behind.

After just two days, Caillié began to suffer from the heat and the wind. His clothes were heavy with sand, and his lips were parched and cracked; thirst tortured him, and the hot desert sand burned his feet. But the Sahara's fiery interior still lay ahead of him.

As his journey continued, the sun became hotter, and water grew scarcer. Caillié dreamed of tinkling brooks and cool refreshing rivers. He tried to buy water but soon found that it was more precious than anything he had to offer in exchange.

Eventually, the plight of the caravan became desperate, and messengers rode ahead to bring back water from the next well. Three days later, they returned gasping with thirst. The well had dried up completely. To survive the return journey, the messengers had killed a camel and drunk the foul-tasting slime in its stomach.

Finally, when Caillié had almost given up hope, the caravan reached the oasis of Telig. There drifting sand had filled the wells, and before they could drink, the exhausted travelers had to dig down to reach the water. Maddened by thirst, the camels fought them for a drink. Caillié was so thirsty that when a pool formed in the sand, he squirmed between the camel's legs and plunged his face into the water.

Caillié's nightmare trip through the desert lasted nearly 12 weeks, but he was still not safe when it was over. His disguise, convincing in the south, did not so easily fool the Arabs of Morocco. The weary explorer faced another barrage of suspicious questions before he could continue his journey.

At last, in September 1829, Caillié stumbled into the office of a French official in Tangier. Filthy, ragged, and starving, he looked like a beggar.

"I am a Frenchman," he gasped. "I have been to Timbuktu!"

RENE CAILLIE'S ROUTE
The French explorer struggled through rain forest, trudged across highlands, and trekked through deserts on his epic journey. His route took him roughly northeast from the coast of Sierra Leone, through Guinea and Mali to Timbuktu. He then headed north, traveling through Algeria

Apart from thirst, desert travelers also feared bandits and sandstorms. For protection, many joined a camel caravan led by people with much experience in this harsh environment.

THE RANI OF JHANSI

The story so far...

In 1853, the Maharaja of Jhansi lay dying. His son was too young to take his place, so the maharaja decided that his wife, Lakshmi Bai, should rule Jhansi. But after his death, the British, who already ruled much of India, announced that they would control Jhansi. Lakshmi Bai was furious. "I will not give up my Jhansi!" she shouted—but she could do little about it. Then, in 1857, there was a rebellion against British rule. In Jhansi, Lakshmi Bai led the revolt.

THE FIGHTING PRINCESS Lakshmi Bai (1830–57) was the rani (princess or maharani) of Jhansi, a small state in northern India. Before she married the maharaja (prince), she had grown up in his palace. With her adopted brothers, she had learned to debate, to ride horses and elephants, and to handle weapons.

LAKSHMI BAI, THE RANI OF JHANSI, knew that the British were coming to stop the rebellion. She quickly prepared her defenses. Some 14,000 fighters volunteered, and she set them to work strengthening Jhansi's crumbling fort, casting new cannons, and preparing supplies.

The rani was ready, but so too were her British foes. By March 23rd, they had reached Jhansi and almost surrounded it. The British officers saw that they would not win a swift victory. The fort was raised on a rock. Its walls were nearly 16 feet (5 meters) thick and twice as high.

BOOM! British guns opened fire. Day after day, they pounded the fort. The rebels inside fought back valiantly under the rani's command. Everyone helped. The British soldiers saw the women of Jhansi carrying ammunition and working in the gun emplacements. Some spotted the rani herself shooting from a high white turret. She was easy to spot because she wore a white silk blouse with white trousers and a long tunic. A diamond-studded sword was tucked into her wide belt.

Each day, British cannonballs smashed holes in the walls. But each night, the women of Jhansi plugged the gaps with timber and earth. After a week, the British began to run out of ammunition. The bombardment had failed, but the siege of Jhansi was not yet over.

The final battle for the town began before dawn on April 3rd. As the British crept through the darkness towards the fort, bugle calls sounded the alarm. The rani rode around the walls on a white horse, directing the defense, but the volunteers were no match for the well-trained British army. In ten minutes, the British troops had fought their way

through cannonballs, musket fire, and rockets, and were over the wall. The fighting became even more ferocious as the soldiers battled hand to hand on the parapet.

The rani fought alongside her warriors, and together they beat off the attack. But it was only a temporary victory. Soon the British returned and set fire to the town. When the rani realized that she could not save her beloved Jhansi, she decided to flee. She dressed in armor and equipped herself with a dagger and two revolvers. Then she wrapped her baby son in a silk shawl so that she could carry him on her back. At midnight, she escaped, riding so swiftly that no one could follow. Within a day, she had galloped to safety in the rebel-held Kalpi fortress, 100 miles (160 kilometers) away.

She was among friends again, and with her allies, she plotted the capture of the nearby fortress stronghold of Gwalior.

The bold plan succeeded. In the safety of Gwalior castle, one of the rebel leaders, Rao Sahib, was crowned a prince. The coronation was an excuse for wild rejoicing, but the rani was worried. She warned her people not to forget that they were in grave danger.

Sure enough, British troops were soon massing outside the great fortress. And, just as the rani had feared, the defenders were unprepared. When the attack came, the rani knew it might be her last battle. She cropped her hair like a man's, buckled on her armor, and picked up her jeweled sword. Finally, she put on heavy gold anklets and the priceless pearl necklace of Scindia from the treasury of Gwalior.

The battle was swift and decisive. By the second day, it was clear that the rebels could not hold the fort. The rani led her troops out to block the roads leading into Gwalior. On hilly ground, she faced a cavalry charge.

The rani fought like a demon. Holding the reins of her horse in her teeth, she swung a sword in each hand. But, in the desperate battle, she did not see a British hussar taking careful aim with his carbine. His shot killed her instantly.

IN THE YEARS THAT FOLLOWED...

The rani of Jhansi had been among the most dangerous of India's rebel leaders. Even the British commanders saluted "her bravery, cleverness, and perseverance." Her death helped Britain to recover control of India, but it also made Lakshmi Bai a legend. Today, she is still India's "Warrior Queen."

British soldiers attacked the fort of Gwalior, nearly 62 miles (100 km) from Jhansi.

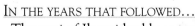

WEAPONS
The jewel-encrusted swords with which the rani fought were signs of her royal status. Beautifully decorated weapons like this dagger were rarely used in warfare. Most often, they were worn as jewelry. Even plain fighting swords were cherished for their craftsmanship. As early as the first century, Indian swordsmiths were making fine weapons and exporting them to Africa.

THE FATAL DESERT CROSSING

The story so far…

In the summer of 1860, a committee in the Australian colony of Victoria planned a grand expedition. Its aim was to cross central Australia's unexplored desert to reach the north coast and to return overland. The committee chose Robert Burke to be the expedition leader. Burke recruited a team of explorers, and he imported camels from India. On August 20th, the expedition left Melbourne with plenty of supplies and all the latest equipment.

Robert Burke   *William Wills*

THE EXPLORATION TEAM Irish-born Robert O'Hara Burke (1820–61) was a police superintendent. He had no special survival skills and no knowledge of exploration. But his good family background helped him beat experienced explorers to the job of leading an expedition across Australia. He chose Englishman William Wills (1834–61) as surveyor and astronomer. He also asked odd-job man Charles Gray (c.1818–61) to join the expedition at Menindee on the way north, and John King (1841–72) was hired as the camel-handler's assistant.

THE EXPLORERS HAD BARELY LEFT MELBOURNE before trouble began. The heavily laden carts and pack animals moved very slowly. The horses fought with the camels, and the humans in the party also found it hard to get along with one another. Furthermore, their bossy leader, Robert Burke, lacked one quality that every explorer needs: a good sense of direction! Even on short trips, he frequently lost his way.

Burke argued with the expedition's foreman and fired him. Then both his second-in-command and his doctor quit. In October, the rest of the team reached the town of Menindee, where Burke hurried to rearrange the expedition.

He would have to travel faster. Rival explorer John McDouall Stuart was rumored to have left South Australia on a similar mission. The expedition had become a competition.

Burke's plan was to make his expedition team smaller, leaving behind half its members in Menindee. With just seven companions, he could race to the Indian Ocean.

At first, the plan worked. In little more than three weeks, Burke and his chosen companions had reached the halfway point at Cooper Creek. They camped in the cool shade of gum trees and splashed in the muddy water.

It was a welcome relief after the dry plains that they had trekked through, but it was not an ideal base.

Black flies swarmed everywhere and hundreds of rats ate their supplies—not just their food but even their shoe leather and equipment.

Burke stayed at Cooper Creek for a month, while he searched for tracks and water further north. But every one of his excursions ended in failure. A parched, scorching plain stretched to the horizon.

Finally, Burke decided to split the team again. Three men would wait at Cooper Creek; he would hurry on with Charles Gray, William Wills, and John King.

As Burke's group trudged north, they met Aborigines, who gave them food and showed them how to find water.

But Burke and the rest of the men distrusted the Aborigines and had little respect for their knowledge of the hot, dry outback.

On the flat plains, the expedition made good progress, and Burke was eager to keep up the pace. So when they reached the Selwyn Mountains, he decided to go straight over them. The climb alarmed the camels, and Burke wrote in his journal that they were "bleeding, sweating, and groaning" after the crossing.

Worse still, the rainy season was beginning. A month before, the hike across the land north of the mountains would have been easy. But because of the earlier delays, Burke and his small party had to continue their journey in tropical storms. The rain soaked the dusty ground, and the men and animals wallowed in sticky mud.

Nevertheless, by the end of January, they were tantalizingly close to their target. Once again, Burke decided that he would make faster progress with a smaller group. So, leaving behind Gray and King, he and Wills dashed for the Gulf of Carpentaria on the north coast. By February 10th, almost six months after leaving Melbourne, they were close enough to the sea to smell it. Surely, they were only a day away from swimming in pounding surf.

Like many Europeans at that time, Burke and Wills scorned the Aborigines, who knew how to find food and water in the harsh outback. Aborigines collected fruits, nuts, and grubs, and hunted animals, such as kangaroos, with spears and boomerangs unchanged for thousands of years.

THE ENDLESS OUTBACK Inland from Australia's fertile coastal areas lies nearly 1.5 million square miles (4 million square kilometers) of dry, empty country—the outback. It has scarcely changed since Burke's expedition trudged wearily across it nearly a century and a half ago. Much of the land is absolutely flat with few landmarks to guide travelers.

No palm-fringed beach lined the shore of the Gulf of Carpentaria. Instead, tropical woodland gradually merged with sea water. Although the explorers waded through the tangled mangrove swamp, they never saw the open ocean. It was a disappointment, but at least they had reached their target, and besides, Burke had other things to worry about. Had he really been the first? Or had Stuart reached the ocean before he had? Could they survive the long trek back to Cooper Creek?

Burke and Wills returned to their waiting companions, and the four men set off south. The journey north had taken eight weeks; they had just five weeks' worth of rations left for the return trip.

To their meager food supplies, the men added any animals they could catch—even insects—and any plants that looked edible. Once, Burke became ill after eating a snake.

Hunger soon set the four men against each other. When Wills caught Gray stealing flour from the rations, Burke beat the thief.

CREEKS AND BILLABONGS
Following rain, outback rivers and lakes seem to appear from nowhere, then dry up and disappear just as suddenly. Survival may depend on spotting signs of water, such as circling birds many miles away.

When their flour and biscuits ran out, the men ate their horses. Even with this extra food, Gray became so weak that he had to be tied onto his camel. Just 70 miles (112 kilometers) short of Cooper Creek, he died.

His starving, exhausted companions dug his grave with the only suitable tools they had—their bare hands. But this final tribute to Gray delayed the three remaining men by a whole day.

Three days later, they saw the welcome outline of Cooper Creek on the horizon. They'd made it! In minutes they'd be embracing their friends! They'd plunge into the creek and soothe their parched throats with its water. In just a few weeks, perhaps, they'd be back in Melbourne!

But something was not quite right. As Burke, Wills, and King drew closer, they looked for figures under the trees. There was nobody there.

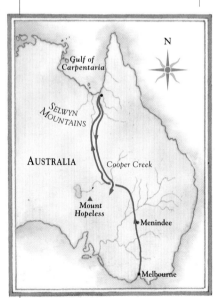

ACROSS THE DESERT
From Melbourne, on Australia's lush southeast coast, Burke led his men almost directly north to the Gulf of Carpentaria, 1,400 miles (2,250 kilometers) away. The men then attempted to return the same way.

They croaked out greetings. But there were no replies. After a frantic search of the deserted camp, Wills saw a message carved on a tree.

DIG 3 FT NW. APR 21 1861

"April 21st?" he thought. "That's today!"

The three men scraped at the loose soil. Two feet (half a meter) down was a box of supplies, and underneath that was a message sealed in a bottle. They read it with dismay. Their three comrades had left the camp just eight hours earlier, but Burke, Wills, and King knew that they would never catch up with them on their two weak camels.

Burke decided not to try. Instead, the three men headed for the nearest European settlement, 150 miles (240 kilometers) south at Mount Hopeless. It was a fatal mistake. Their clothes turned to rags, their rations were soon finished, and they were further weakened by thirst.

After two months, Wills could walk no further and urged his two companions to go on without him. A few days later, Burke died. When King returned to look for Wills, he too was dead. Alone in the outback, King turned for help to the Aborigines whom he had once rejected.

An ominous message was buried with the supplies.

They sheltered and fed him until a search party arrived two months later. At first, his rescuers did not recognize him.

"Who in the name of wonder are you?" one asked.

The starving, sunburned figure replied, "I am King, sir…the last man of the exploring expedition."

WHAT HAPPENED NEXT…

Burke need not have raced so dangerously across Australia. Although no one in Melbourne knew it until months later, Stuart's expedition had failed before Burke and his team had even started. The return of King caused a sensation at first, but the humble camel handler was soon forgotten. In contrast, a monument was built in memory of the bumbling, gentleman-hero Burke and his faithful companion Wills. It still stands in Melbourne today.

ABORIGINAL LAND

The Aborigines are thought to have lived in Australia for more than 40,000 years. Their traditional skills allowed them to find food and water in apparently empty and hostile regions. At night, smoky fires were lit to keep their brush shelters (like the one above) warm and free of biting insects.

> " *Nothing now but the greatest good luck can save any of us.* "
>
> WILLIAM WILLS

NED KELLY'S LAST STAND

The story so far...

In June 1880, Ned Kelly and his gang were on the run after robbing banks in Victoria, Australia. They shot three policemen who had been sent to capture them, and took refuge in the small village of Glenrowan. The four men knew that a police train would be sent after them, so, on Sunday, June 27th, they tore up the railroad track close to the village. Then they waited in a nearby hotel for the train to crash. Sympathizers joined the gang, and they took other villagers hostage.

THE OUTLAW
Edward "Ned" Kelly (1855–80) grew up to be the most famous of Australia's outlaws. These bandits lived by robbing travelers and settlers on the thinly populated land outside of the coastal cities.

ALL THROUGH SUNDAY, THE GANG WAITED FOR THE TRAIN. When evening came, Ned Kelly's brother Dan suggested fleeing, but Ned refused. "I'm tired of running," he said. So the four men waited and passed the time drinking and dancing with the villagers.

By the early hours of Monday, even Ned was ready to leave. But first, he jumped on a chair and began a lecture about the gang's exploits and hatred for the police. The sound of an approaching train interrupted him. It was the police! But instead of speeding through the station, hitting the broken track, and crashing into a ravine as the gang had planned, the train was stopping. Ned guessed that the gang had been betrayed.

In fact, it was the village schoolmaster who had stopped the train. He had improvised a warning light by holding his wife's red shawl in front of a candle.

"They're coming here. We'll have to stand and fight!" Ned shouted to his comrades when he saw armed police creeping up to surround the hotel.

From the windows, the gang saw shadowy figures approaching in the moonlight. Ned crept outside and opened fire. Immediately, the police fired back, and the village was filled with gunfire and the screams of the terrified villagers inside the hotel. When there was a break in the shooting, the Kelly gang cursed the police and threw down a bold challenge. "Come on! Fire away, you'll never harm us." Then the gunfire began again.

At dawn, a tall figure loomed out of the mist behind the ring of police surrounding the hotel. One startled policemen thought it was the bunyip, a swamp monster from the legends of native Australian people called Aborigines. Another guessed it was one of the gang.

"He's covered with iron," the policeman called out.

The officer was right. It was Ned. Under his gray coat, he wore rough armor made of the iron from farm plows. When the siege had begun, gunfire had stopped him from returning to the hotel, and he had hidden in a gully until daybreak. Now he was striding calmly toward the police, firing his revolver, while nine police guns were firing back at him.

Ned hesitated as each bullet struck, but he continued to advance. He laughed at his foes and defiantly tapped his revolver on his armor to show that the bullets could not harm him. But one policeman noticed Ned's unprotected feet and shot at them. As Ned staggered to keep his balance, a chink opened in the armor. The officer took careful aim at Ned's exposed thigh.

Ned's armor weighed 97 pounds (44 kilograms) including his helmet.

His shot brought down the ironclad giant.

"I'm done!" Ned called out.

The policemen rushed to catch him. They stripped off his armor and saw that he was bleeding heavily from his wounds.

Meanwhile the siege continued. It ended only when the police set fire to the hotel, burning the remaining two members of the gang. Police bullets had already killed the fourth.

Ned stood trial and was found guilty of murdering a policeman. He was hanged on November 11, 1880.

A police bullet wounded Ned's left foot.

NED KELLY'S CAPTORS
After the gunfight, the policemen who captured Kelly posed for the camera, but it was Ned himself who was seen as the real hero. Although he had robbed and killed, common people admired him for standing up to the wealthy and powerful. Like Ned, many ordinary Australians had convict parents. They did not like the police, who they believed drove Kelly to commit his crimes.

NED'S HOMEMADE ARMOR
Crudely made from iron plows, Ned's armor covered his chest, stomach, back, and the tops of his thighs. A heavy helmet shaped like a tin can protected his head. However, there was no protection for his hands, arms, and legs, where he was hit by many shotgun pellets. Although bullets bounced off the helmet, their impact bruised Ned's face badly. A doctor who examined Kelly found that two bullets and half a dozen shotgun pellets had hit him. But Australian folklore exaggerated his strength: according to outlaw legend, it took 28 wounds to bring him down.

AN AFRICAN ADVENTURE

The story so far...

At a time when few European women traveled abroad alone, Mary Kingsley set off for the west coast of Africa. She chose to travel with only African guides, which was also unusual for a European in 1893. Mary's party explored far inland, wading across swamps, navigating rapids, and braving crocodiles, leeches, and insects as big as "flying lobsters." When Mary traveled between the Ogooué and Rembwe Rivers, she stayed in a village belonging to the Fang people, who she believed were cannibals.

A DETERMINED WOMAN
After her mother and father died in 1892, the determined Englishwoman Mary Kingsley (1862–1900) went in search of adventure. With a revolver, goods to trade, and wearing a thick woolen skirt and a high-necked blouse, she sailed for what is now Gabon in West Africa. On her return, she became famous by writing about her adventures.

MARY COULD NOT SLEEP. Through the thin walls of her palm-leaf hut, she could hear the agonized howling of a leopard. She had seen it when she arrived at the village earlier that day. It was fighting to free itself from a snare in which it had been caught by accident. The enraged animal was much too dangerous to approach, and the villagers were keeping their distance and letting it use up its strength by thrashing around all night in the trap.

But the beast's cries tormented Mary. She crept out into the night barefoot and picked her way gingerly though the undergrowth to avoid the snakes and stinging insects. The animal's roars made it easy for her to find the trap even though it was dark. Before she could make out the leopard's shape in the blackness, she saw its brilliant eyes staring at her.

Mary's hut had a roof of thatched palm leaves and walls made from palm-leaf mats.

The Ogooué River is surrounded by dense rain forest.

Mary pitied the animal and wanted to release it, but she was wary of its deadly teeth and claws. Eventually, she thought of a plan.

The trap was held in place by several stakes hammered into the ground. The leopard was not strong enough to force them out. So Mary decided to pull out all the stakes except for one, then flee, leaving the animal to uproot the last one by itself.

She set to work at this dangerous scheme. But then she stepped too close to the snarling cat.

It slashed her skirt with its razor-sharp claws. Startled but unhurt, she continued until she had succeeded in uprooting all but one of the stakes.

As she had expected, the leopard twisted and heaved, pulling out the final stake by itself. But Mary could not run away as she had hoped. The freed leopard moved quickly toward her and circled, sniffing close enough for her to feel its hot breath on her skin. For a moment, she was absolutely terrified. Then her self-assurance returned.

"Go home, you fool!" she commanded the circling beast. The leopard stopped and stared at Mary. Then, obediently, it turned and slunk away.

Almost as soon as its long tail had disappeared into the jungle, Mary heard a rustling behind her. A figure suddenly dropped down from the trees.

The leopard is one of Africa's most dangerous predators.

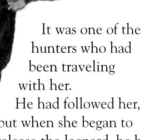

It was one of the hunters who had been traveling with her.

He had followed her, but when she began to release the leopard, he had climbed a tree in fear. Now he threw himself at her feet.

He had mistaken her fearlessness for supernatural powers.

"Who but a goddess," he asked Mary, "would dare to command obedience from such a dangerous beast?"

TRAVELING UPRIVER
Mary traveled up the Ogooué River in a dugout canoe. Her journey took her to parts of Africa that no other European had explored.

A snout fish from the Ogooué River preserved in alcohol

FISH COLLECTION
Apart from adventure, the purpose of Mary's trip was the study of fish and insects. She discovered eight new species of fish, three of which were named after her.

TO THE ENDS OF THE EARTH AND BEYOND

WHEN THE 20TH CENTURY BEGAN, only one continent remained unexplored—Antarctica. After the South Pole gave up its icy secrets in 1911, where could adventurers look for fame, danger, and excitement? Only upwards, and that's exactly where many of them headed. Up into the cold blue sky in flying machines. Up the world's highest mountains, where the air is so thin that climbers have to carry their own oxygen. And up farther still, beyond the atmosphere, into orbit and into space— all the way to the Moon.

These daring adventurers only became famous after reaching their goals. Until then, they were ordinary people from ordinary families. Yuri Gagarin, the first person in space, was a farm boy. Climber Edmund Hillary was a beekeeper. Aviator Amelia Earhart was a social worker. With determination and daring, anybody can be an adventurer. So who will be the next great adventurers, and where will they go?

As they headed for the Moon's surface, unexpected problems faced the two men inside the fragile space craft in "The First Moon Landing."

RACE TO THE SOUTH POLE

The story so far...

Polar exploration made news headlines in 1911. Robert Scott in Britain and Roald Amundsen in Norway were both planning expeditions—apparently to opposite ends of the earth. Both explorers set off the same month. But when Scott reached Australia, he learned that Amundsen had changed his plans. Now his target was the South Pole, too. Scott's scientific expedition had turned into a race.

Robert Scott   *Roald Amundsen*

POLAR EXPLORERS

In 1901, English naval officer Robert Scott (1868–1912) led an expedition to the unexplored southern continent of Antarctica. He was determined that the first person to reach the South Pole would be an Englishman. In 1909, he announced plans to lead his own scientific expedition all the way to the South Pole. Norwegian Roald Amundsen (1872–1928) gave up a career in medicine to become a sailor and explorer. He hoped to be the first to reach the North Pole. When another explorer beat him to this goal, he sought a different challenge.

IT WAS JANUARY 1911. The two expeditions reached Antarctica within days of each other. Although they shared the same destination, they had different plans. Amundsen's team would ski to the Pole, and dogs would pull sleds bearing food and equipment. Scott mistrusted dogs, so he only took a few, and his men were poor skiers. He planned to use ponies and motorized sleds to haul most of the equipment.

Scott's problems began as soon as he unloaded his ship. A motorized sled and seven ponies were lost when they crashed through the ice.

Before the polar winter began in April, each team needed to create supply bases along the route to the Pole. Scott managed to ferry one ton of food and fuel south—barely enough for his 16-man expedition. Amundsen had more luck. His men unloaded three tons of supplies for their team of just five men.

In October, the race began. Without radio, neither team knew which had started first.

Scott's English team sent out an advance party on the motorized sleds. But they did not get far before the sleds broke down. Lacking vital spares, the drivers abandoned them and continued on foot. The main party, with Scott in command, soon found the sleds and, ten days later, caught up with their drivers.

Amundsen's Norwegians, meanwhile, had crossed the Transantarctic mountains. On the other side, they shot their spare dogs, feeding some of the meat to the 18 that remained and feasting on the rest of the meat themselves.

Across the ice, 350 miles (560 kilometers) away, the English explorers were determined to press on, but their ponies were sick and starving. Scott picked four of the men to accompany him to the Pole. The rest returned to their base camp.

Hunched against the snow, Scott and his four companions trudged south. The men now had to haul the heavy sleds themselves. They thought of Amundsen constantly. Was he in the lead? Would they beat him to the Pole?

Doubts plagued Amundsen too. One of his team noticed a dog sniffing the breeze coming from the Pole. Perhaps the animal could smell the English team ahead.

On December 15th, the Norwegian dog drivers cracked their whips with renewed enthusiasm. The Pole lay just over the horizon. But would there be a British flag flapping in the icy wind? Soon, the Norwegian navigators calculated that they were at the very bottom of the Earth. "Halt!" they cried out. There was not a flag in sight, just powdery snow. They'd done it! They feasted on chocolate and seal steak, and snapped a photograph. Before turning for home, they marked the Pole with flags. They also left a letter to the King of Norway with a note asking Scott to deliver the letter if they did not return.

A month later, Scott's weary, hungry team trudged up to the Norwegian flags. Bitterly disappointed, Scott wrote in his diary, "Great God! This is an awful place…."

But Scott's return journey was to be more awful still. Exhausted and starving, the five men became weaker and weaker. After a month, one of the team died from hunger and cold. After another month, frostbite made Titus Oates lame. Realizing that he was slowing everyone down, he walked out into the snow to die. But Oates's sacrifice was not enough to save his companions. A blizzard trapped them in their tent. Their food, fuel, and strength were exhausted, and the unlucky explorers died.

IN THE YEARS THAT FOLLOWED…

Amundsen returned home to Norway, where he received a quiet welcome. In England, however, the tragic news of Scott's failed attempt to reach the Pole soon made the English explorer a legend.

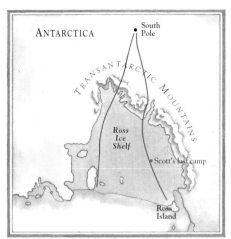

ANTARCTICA — South Pole — TRANSANTARCTIC MOUNTAINS — Ross Ice Shelf — Scott's last camp — Ross Island

➤ Amundsen's route, 1911–12

➤ Scott's route, 1911–12

TWO ROUTES TO THE POLE
Amundsen and Scott each had bases on the sea ice around 850 miles (1,350 km) from the South Pole. Crossing the ice and climbing the Transantarctic mountains took them onto the high polar plateau for the final dash to the Pole. Both teams then intended to retrace their steps back to their bases.

"Victory awaits those who have everything in order—people call that luck."

ROALD AMUNDSEN

THE RED BARON

The story so far...

Across the World War I battlefields of northern France, the German and English troops faced each other from muddy trenches (fortified ditches). Barbed-wire and machine guns made advancing impossible, so the battle was fought in the skies above. In light aircraft made of timber and canvas, brave fliers hunted each other in deadly dogfights.

WALKING ACROSS THE WINDSWEPT AIRFIELD, Manfred von Richthofen chatted and laughed with his fellow pilots. It was a fine day, and he was looking forward to the afternoon's flying. He climbed into the cockpit and started the engine. His plane soared into the sky, and soon the airfield was just a muddy strip far below. Within an hour, he spotted three fighters. Squinting into the bright sun, Richthofen identified them as De Haviland DH2s. British! They were too high to attack, but he could tell from the way they flew that, like him, they were keen for a fight. Richthofen knew it was only a matter of time before one of the aircraft saw him and gave chase. Sure enough, the enemy aircraft split up. One dived toward him, and the pilot opened fire.

THE DAREDEVIL PILOT German airman Manfred von Richthofen (1892–1918) came from a wealthy family. Even as a boy, he was a daredevil. At the age of ten, he climbed a church spire and tied a handkerchief to the lightning conductor. He went to military school from the age of 11, and in 1915, he joined Germany's Imperial Air Service as a fighter pilot.

Startled, Richthofen turned his plane to avoid the burst of bullets. The DH2 banked steeply to follow him. It was an even match. Richthofen did not know it, but he had picked a fight with one of Britain's best pilots. Major Lanoe Hawker had shot down nine German aircraft and had been awarded his country's highest military medal for bravery.

The two aircraft began a corkscrew chase. Neither could get close enough behind the other to open fire. And neither dared pull out of the circle, for each knew his foe would follow and shoot him down. Faster and faster they flew. At first, Richthofen counted the circles, but at 50 he gave up. He knew he had plenty of fuel and a strong wind on his side.

With each circle, the wind blew them deeper over German territory. Soon the British pilot would not have enough fuel to return home. Finally, Hawker's nerve broke. His plane darted from the circling combat. Richthofen was close behind. As the planes skimmed the treetops, the German squeezed the trigger of his machine guns. By zigzagging, the British plane avoided the bullets. Then, just as Richthofen had the DH2 in his gunsights, his weapons jammed. He was unarmed. Worse still, Hawker was getting away!

Richthofen tried his guns once more. They fired, and his heart pounded with relief. Ahead of him, the British aircraft crashed to the ground. The German flying ace had won another victory. He returned home triumphant.

What happened next…

Over the next 17 months, Richthofen shot down another 69 aircraft. He became a German hero, winning the country's Blue Max medal. The squadron that he commanded flew aircraft painted red, and he soon earned his famous nickname—the Red Baron.

Richthofen risked death every time he flew. On April 21, 1917, in his eagerness to claim his 81st victim, he became reckless. He was chasing a British aircraft, a Sopwith Camel, and was gaining fast. But the pilot's erratic flying made him a difficult target. The wind blew Richthofen's triplane into enemy territory. His aircraft was raked with fire from an enemy plane and an antiaircraft battery on the ground. The Red Baron was killed by a single bullet.

German machine guns fired between the propeller blades, but the simpler British guns could not do this, so British pilots had to sit in front of the propeller.

THE BLUE MAX
On January 4, 1917, Richthofen shot down his 16th enemy aircraft, making him Germany's top pilot. The German emperor rewarded him with the country's highest military medal, inscribed *pour le Mérite* (for merit). The award's blue enamel badge earned it the name Blue Max.

When Richthofen's bright red triplane crashed to the ground, troops seeking morbid souvenirs tore it to pieces.

FLYING NONSTOP TO PARIS

When hotel tycoon Raymond Orteig offered a $25,000 prize for the first nonstop flight between New York and Paris, Charles Lindbergh decided to try to win it. In 1926, he had a special aircraft built. Most of his competitors were using planes with three engines and a crew of at least two; Lindbergh could afford only one engine and had to fly alone to make room for the fuel tanks. As he prepared for takeoff, he knew that he was risking his life.

A PASSION FOR FLIGHT
American aviation pioneer Charles Lindbergh (1902–74) left college to learn to fly. When World War I (1914–18) ended, the United States armed forces sold their surplus aircraft, and Lindbergh was able to buy his first plane. With it, he began a career carrying air mail and giving flying lessons. He also worked as a stunt pilot. Aircraft were still such a novelty that crowds paid to watch his daring flying displays. His attempt to fly across the Atlantic Ocean on May 20–21, 1927 changed his life forever.

LINDBERGH'S AIRCRAFT, THE *SPIRIT OF ST. LOUIS*, was tiny—just 28 feet (8.5 meters) long, the length of a tour bus. Highly flammable aviation fuel, needed for the long flight, filled tanks in the wings and the fuselage (the main body of the plane). The biggest tank was in front of the cockpit, blocking the pilot's view. To see where he was going, Lindbergh had to either use a periscope or lean out the window.

On the rain-swept runway, Lindbergh leaned out the cockpit window. "Contact!" he shouted. His mechanic spun the propeller to start the engine. It was the most dangerous moment in the young pilot's life. If he crashed, the full fuel tanks would explode, killing him instantly. Crashes had already killed four pilots trying for the Orteig prize. But he couldn't hesitate now: Two other competitors were readying their aircraft.

The *Spirit of St. Louis* began to bump along the grass runway, slowly gathering speed. Lindbergh pulled back on the joystick. He was airborne!

Lindbergh's worries about takeoff were far behind him, when 13 hours later, he realized that he had a new problem. Flying through a cloud, he had glanced at the wing. It was covered in ice! If the coating grew thicker, it would slow the plane. Fighting panic, Lindbergh turned and flew out of the cloud. To save weight, he had not loaded a parachute, and if his fuel ran out too soon, he would plunge into the icy Atlantic with his plane.

Finally, after checking the wing every few minutes, he was sure that the ice had stopped forming. He'd have to avoid the clouds from now on, though detours would waste precious fuel.

Lindbergh's energy began to run out. He fought off sleep, but he found it hard to tell where dreams ended and reality began. Each time he dozed, the plane drifted dangerously off course.

Lindbergh shook himself awake. He had been flying for 27 hours, and he had no idea where he was. Then suddenly, he saw changes in the ocean below. A porpoise leaped. A seagull circled.

To his delight, he saw fishing boats. He must be near land. He brought the plane down until it almost touched the waves, then he cut the throttle to silence the engine. From the cockpit, he bellowed, "Which way is Ireland?"

The fishermen just stared. They could not hear him. Fearing that he would crash into the sea, Lindbergh climbed again and flew on.

Minutes later, he saw land. But where was he? He hadn't expected to be flying over Ireland for nearly three hours. Was he dreaming? He looked at his charts and soon matched the coast to a line on the map. It was southwest Ireland! Lindbergh banked the plane and flew in a lazy circle, taking in every detail of the brilliant green farmland. He circled twice more, then leveled out and glanced again at the map. But when he looked up, the land had disappeared! All he could see ahead was ocean and cloud stretching all the way to the horizon.

Lindbergh kept himself calm. "There is always a simple answer when life seems as wrong as this," he thought, and he looked back over his shoulder. Ireland lay directly behind him. Now he was heading back toward America! Banking to turn back on course, he flew over Ireland and on over England. Soon, he would be above France, and by midnight, he would have reached his destination—Paris.

When Lindbergh landed, a crowd of around 25,000 people broke steel fences and rushed a police barrier. A sea of hands lifted the weary aviator off the ground and carried him high above the crowd. Lindbergh was now famous.

ATLANTIC CROSSING
It took Lindbergh 33½ hours to fly across the Atlantic from New York to Paris. Today, a supersonic jet can complete the same journey in just 3 hours.

GOODWILL GESTURE
Lindbergh later made a series of flights over Europe and America to please his fans.

THE GREAT AIR DERBY

The story so far...

Amelia Earhart wanted to repeat her famous flight across the Atlantic Ocean—this time as a solo pilot. But she knew that she'd need more flying experience before she could attempt it safely. In 1929, Amelia helped organize an all-women "air derby," or air race, across the United States. The race would give her just the practice she needed. Competitors would fly from Santa Monica, California, to Cleveland, Ohio, in nine one-day stages. The winner would be the pilot with the lowest total flying time.

WORLD-FAMOUS FLYING ACE
After her first flight in 1920, American social worker Amelia Earhart (1897–1937) became obsessed with flying. She immediately signed up for lessons, paying for them by selling sausages. She soon bought her own plane, and in 1922, she flew higher than any woman had ever flown before. She became famous as the first woman to cross the Atlantic Ocean by air—even though she traveled only as a passenger.

AMELIA KNEW THAT SHE WOULD BE COMPETING against better pilots than herself, but she was sure she could beat them if she had a fast enough aircraft.

She bought the fastest available—a Lockheed Vega. This big transport plane was unlike anything that she had flown before. Another pilot warned her that the Vega was "unstable and tricky near the ground." Just how tricky, Amelia would soon find out.

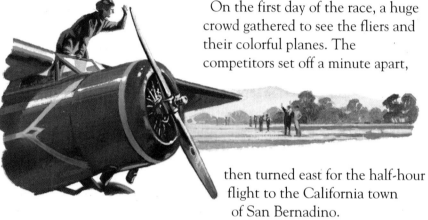

On the first day of the race, a huge crowd gathered to see the fliers and their colorful planes. The competitors set off a minute apart, then turned east for the half-hour flight to the California town of San Bernadino.

Amelia wasn't among the leaders. Engine problems delayed her, and she arrived long after most of the others.

On the second day, the pilots faced a long flight to Phoenix, Arizona. They would have to find their way across scorching deserts using compasses and road maps.

Rumors of sabotage made everyone nervous. Suspicions deepened when a mechanic poured oil into the fuel tank of an aircraft. However, the mistake was fixed, and at dawn, the planes soared into the sky.

Amelia's luck had turned. She made up the time that she had lost and raced into the lead. However, the Vega was not easy to fly, and the big engine gave off a lot of heat, making the cockpit uncomfortable. She was relieved when she spotted the desert airstrip where the competitors were landing to refuel. Amelia angled her plane for the final approach. Below her, the parched ground shimmered in the heat. Pushing the joystick forward, Amelia dived toward the landing strip.

Just as she had been warned, the Vega was unstable near the ground. She struggled to control the unwieldy plane. Too late, she realized that the heat had thinned the air, making the big aircraft seem even heavier.

The Vega's tires bounced and squealed as it landed. Amelia braked frantically, but the plane was moving too fast!

She had to fight to keep the plane rolling in a straight line. But where was the runway? Wind had blown sand across it, and heat haze blurred its edges. Suddenly, one of the wheels left the runway and the plane skidded sideways. With an abrupt lurch, the cockpit tilted violently, and the plane bumped to a halt.

Amelia clambered shaken but unhurt from the cockpit. The crash had bent a propeller beyond repair. Her heart sank; was she out of the race?

But the other pilots supported her. They agreed to hold up the race until she could get a replacement propeller.

After the repair, Amelia again took the lead, but she fell back when she lost her way. Other contestants had worse problems: One withdrew, suspecting that acid had been poured on her plane; another's plane caught fire; and several crashed.

When the race ended, Amelia was in third place. It was a crushing disappointment for her, but the race itself was a huge success. Before it began, most men had scoffed at women pilots; afterwards many accepted female pilots as equals.

IN THE YEARS THAT FOLLOWED…

Amelia Earhart's experience in the air derby helped prepare her for more daring feats. In 1932, she became the first woman to fly alone across the Atlantic. Five years later, she died when her aircraft crashed into the Pacific during her second attempt to fly around the world.

JEAN BATTEN
At the same time as Amelia Earhart was breaking records, other women were also making historic flights. In 1935, New Zealand pilot Jean Batten (1909–82) made a solo flight from Brazil to Britain. This was not only a first for a woman but set a record for the journey. Jean also set a record flying from Britain to New Zealand, that went unbroken for 44 years.

FOURTEEN-STOP JOURNEY
The competitors stopped to refuel 13 times during the nine-day air derby. It took nine days because at that time aircraft flew slowly. The Lockheed Vega flew at a top speed of only 150 miles per hour (240 kilometers per hour).

THE *KON-TIKI* EXPEDITION

The story so far...

In 1947, Thor Heyerdahl, a Norwegian, built a raft out of balsa wood so that he could recreate the ancient voyages of the South American people. He believed that they had launched similar log rafts 800 years earlier and that they were the ancestors of the present Pacific Islanders. People laughed at Heyerdahl's ideas and were convinced that the raft would sink. But the Norwegian was sure he was right, and now he wanted to prove it.

THE *KON-TIKI* TEAM
Kon-Tiki's crew members were, from left to right: Knut Haugland, Bengt Danielsson, Thor Heyerdahl (the leader), Erik Hesselberg, Torstein Raaby, and Herman Watzinger.

BLACK SMOKE SPURTED FROM THE FUNNEL OF THE TUGBOAT as it left the small Peruvian port of Callao on April 28th. The tug was not a large boat, but it towered over the balsa-log raft that it towed. On board the raft, the crew prepared its clumsy craft for a long voyage. The six men and their parrot aimed to drift with the wind and the tide a quarter of the way around the world to reach the scattered islands of the Pacific.

Once the *Kon-Tiki* was clear of the busy shipping lanes that fringed the coast, the crew untied the tow ropes, and the tug steamed away. Then they hauled up a rough square sail, and their voyage began.

The six men had a lot to learn. They had built their craft using descriptions of ancient South American boats, but no living mariner knew how to sail it. At first, the sail hung limply, and they cursed the lack of wind. But when the wind came, they were not ready for its strength. To steer the raft, they had to heave on a long oar at the stern. They took turns at this exhausting work.

Soon, the men and their raft felt at home in the sea. Although sharks circled the raft, they did not try to harm the crew. For the first ten weeks of the trip, even the weather seemed kind to the *Kon-Tiki*. But then, in early July, dark clouds appeared from the south. Strong winds and towering waves began to lash the fragile craft. Fearing that the vessel would be destroyed, the crew tied everything down and hung on tight. But the raft rode out the storm.

For one member of the crew, though, the heavy seas were no game. A big wave swept the parrot overboard. The loss of their pet saddened and alarmed the men. They knew it could easily have been one of them. From that day on, they all took extra care.

One day, however, their worst fear came true. While Herman, the raft's meteorologist (weather forecaster) was measuring wind speed, a storm

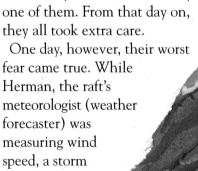

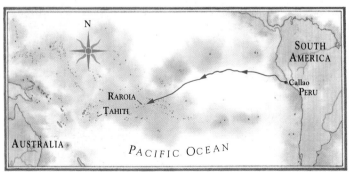

ROUTE OF THE *KON-TIKI* EXPEDITION
Carried more than 5,000 miles (8,000 kilometers) across the Pacific Ocean, the *Kon-Tiki* took advantage of the powerful Peru Current that flows up the west coast of South America.

sucked one of their sleeping bags overboard. Reaching to grab it, Herman lost his balance, slipped on the wet logs, and toppled into the water.

His shouts alerted the rest of the crew, but without a motor they could not stop the *Kon-Tiki*. Herman tried to grab the steering oar but lost his grip. The raft sped past the struggling man. Throwing out a lifeline was useless because the wind just blew it back on board.

Suddenly there was a splash! Knut had plunged into the water with the life preserver. High waves hid him and Herman from view for what seemed like several minutes. Thor and the other crew members held their breath. When the two men finally reappeared, they were both clinging to the life preserver. Their relieved companions hauled in the life preserver and dragged them back on board.

Kon-Tiki *had two masts lashed together and a square sail.*

FLYING FISH
Kon-Tiki's crew feasted on flying fish that stranded themselves on the raft's deck. These fish leap from the water when bigger fish chase them. They can glide for up to half a minute using their enlarged fins like wings.

The crew of the Kon-Tiki could not avoid crashing onto Raroia atoll, which is 21 miles long and 9 miles wide (34 kilometers long and 14.5 kilometers wide).

After three months at sea, the men calculated that land must be nearby. Land birds were beginning to join the sea birds that had been their constant companions. But even by climbing to the top of the mast and straining their eyes, they could not see any low-lying coral islands. They feared they might sail within 12 miles (20 kilometers) of an island and still miss it.

Eventually, it was their ears, not their eyes, that alerted them to land nearby. On July 30th, the screams of land birds made sleep impossible. At daybreak, they could make out a line of land on the horizon. They had done it! The *Kon-Tiki* had proved Thor Heyerdahl right.

Nevertheless, the journey was not over. Landing on the Pacific Islands proved almost as difficult as sailing to them. The ungainly raft drifted onwards. Its crude steering oar was no match for the Pacific swell. Even with the help of islanders who paddled out in long canoes through a gap in the reef (a coral wall that rings many Pacific Island groups), the crew was unable to turn the raft and follow them.

Finally, Torstein spotted another reef ahead. It was too big to steer around, and they were drifting straight toward it.

Kon-Tiki's long journey was going to end in a shipwreck. Thor and his fellow voyagers prepared themselves as best they could. They packed all their most valuable items in waterproof bags and waited for their raft to be smashed to pieces.

As they reached the reef, a massive wave broke over the raft. For a moment, the *Kon-Tiki* was completely submerged. It was all the crew could do to hang on and not be swept overboard. The huge wave subsided, only to be followed by another and another. The mountainous seas crushed the flimsy cabin and smashed the mast. But little by little, the waves drove the raft onto the top of the wide reef.

Eventually, the men jumped from the raft. They salvaged all the equipment they needed and flung it into their rubber life raft, which had floated free of the wreck. Then they waded across a shallow lagoon to a beautiful uninhabited island. Thor Heyerdahl was overwhelmed.

"I sank down on my knees and thrust my fingers deep down in the dry, warm sand," he recalled. His navigator, Bengt, said simply, "Heaven was more or less as I'd imagined it."

BALSA TREES
Thor traveled to the forests of Ecuador to find logs for his craft. The *Kon-Tiki* was made from the trunks of balsa trees. Balsa is a light and buoyant wood well suited to raft building. The logs were floated down river from the forest to the town where Thor and his companions constructed the *Kon-Tiki*.

CORAL ISLAND
After 101 days at sea, the *Kon-Tiki* grounded on a coral reef. Corals are living organisms that form large colonies. In shallow water and over thousands of years, these sea animals build underwater barriers, called reefs, off many coastlines. Sometimes they form a circle, called an atoll.

TO THE SUMMIT OF EVEREST

The story so far...

In spring 1953, an international expedition arrived in Nepal to climb Mount Everest, the world's highest mountain. British climbers led the attempt, but the group also included two climbers from New Zealand and a small group of Sherpas (people of Tibetan origin living on the foothills of the Himalayas). Before the climbers began their attempt, 350 Sherpas helped carry many tons of equipment to Camp 1, located at around 17,900 feet (5,500 meters).

THE CLIMBERS
Nepalese Sherpa Tenzing Norgay (1914–1986) had worked as a porter on many earlier Everest expeditions. He was the *sirdar* (the organizer of porters) for the 1953 expedition. New Zealander Edmund Hillary (b. 1919) was a beekeeper until his 1953 attempt to climb Mount Everest. Since then, he has traveled the world in search of adventure.

THE TEAM SCARCELY PAUSED AT CAMP 1 before tackling one of the most dangerous parts of the expedition—the icefall area of the Khumbu Glacier. This river of ice on Everest's lower slopes moves constantly but very slowly. Its gradual downhill slide fractures the ice into enormous blocks and spikes. To set up camps closer to the summit, the climbers had to find a safe route through this unstable landscape.

They scaled the glacier using traditional ice-climbing methods. Roped together for safety, they cut steps with ice axes. To grip the icy surfaces, they wore crampons (sharp steel spikes) on the soles of their boots.

When deep cracks, known as crevasses, blocked their way, the climbers looked for natural ice bridges across them. They crossed the wider crevasses using a lightweight ladder that they carried up the glacier in three sections. It spanned the widest crevasse with just an arm's length to spare. As Hillary, Tenzing, and three other climbers crept gingerly across this fragile metal bridge, it swayed alarmingly, but held fast. Bridging a huge crevasse on April 25th was an important milestone, and it greatly encouraged the team. The next day, they set off again with renewed enthusiasm and climbed higher still.

But their easy success made Hillary over confident. At the end of the day, he hurried down the now-familiar route towards Camp 1. Roped on behind him, Tenzing had to jog to keep up with the lanky New Zealander. Hillary had just one more narrow crevasse to cross. Although there was an ice bridge, he ignored it, choosing instead to leap exuberantly across the gap. As he landed heavily on the far side, a sharp crack echoed through the snowy stillness. Before he could do anything, Hillary was riding a giant ice block as it tumbled into the blue depths of the glacier.

Instinctively, he straightened his legs, slamming his feet against the side of the crevasse. The spikes of his crampons dug deep into the vertical ice wall, throwing his shoulders back against the other side.

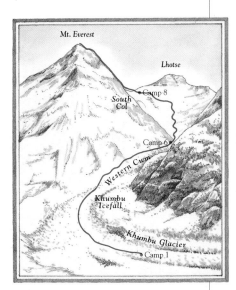

Below him, the block smashed into deadly sharp splinters. But above him, Tenzing quickly secured the safety rope, saving them both from a frozen grave.

As he clambered out of the crevasse, Hillary cursed himself for his foolishness. When he reached the top, he was astonished to see that his calm climbing companion treated the mishap as a great joke!

Two weeks later, the route up the icefall was complete. The expedition leader, John Hunt, called his team together at Camp 1. All eyes were on him as he started to speak. The team was waiting to hear who had been picked to make the final attempts on the summit.

But before reading the list, Hunt outlined the problems that they faced, in particular the low oxygen levels. On high mountains, the air is thin. Lack of oxygen can cause mountain sickness (see p. 52). To avoid this hazard, the climbers would breathe oxygen from tanks on their backs. But there was only enough gas for two attempts.

At last, Hunt read the list of summit climbers. Charles Evans and Tom Bourdillon would lead the first team. Edmund Hillary grinned at Tenzing Norgay when Hunt revealed that they were to lead the second team.

If the other climbers felt disappointed, they forgot about it in the frantic activity of the next two weeks. They had to transport the equipment up the glacier to a string of higher camps.

If Tenzing had not reacted quickly, the safety rope could have dragged him into the crevasse that nearly swallowed Hillary.

ROUTE TO THE TOP
To reach the summit, the British team first had to climb the Khumbu Glacier, which fills the Western Cwm, a bowl-shaped valley on Everest's side. From there, they climbed Lhotse, the mountain next to Everest, to reach South Col, a ridge leading to Everest's

Crampons helped their boots grip the ice.

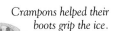

OXYGEN SUPPLIES
The thin air at the top of Everest contains so little oxygen that the climbers had to breathe supplies of the gas from tube-shaped tanks strapped on their backs. The lightest tank weighed more than 11 pounds (5 kilograms). Climbing with the three tanks that they needed was like carrying a six-year-old child up the mountain.

“High above us, almost so far as to be unreal, was the grim black summit of Everest.”
EDMUND HILLARY

SHERPA BAGGAGE TRAIN
There were no roads to Everest, so the expedition's many tons of equipment had to be carried carefully along narrow mountain tracks. Hundreds of Sherpa men and women lugged the loads to a temporary base camp near the remote Buddhist monastery of Thyangboche.

It was a landscape of spectacular beauty and great danger. Crevasses, deep snow, and wind-polished ice made climbing extremely dangerous.

But finally, the two teams and their supplies were ready. Evans and Bourdillon set off for the summit, accompanied by Hunt and two Sherpas. The five men soon disappeared from view.

At Camp 7, Hillary now organized his team, and soon they too were climbing up Everest's snowy shoulders. When they reached the highest camp, Camp 8, the swirling mist that surrounded them cleared briefly.

Crevasses are deep cracks in the ice that coats high mountains. They blocked many of the routes up Everest.

Relays of climbers carried supplies and equipment among the nine camps spread up the mountainside.

“They're up! By God, they're up,” shouted one of Hillary's team. He had spotted Evans and Bourdillon, by now climbing on their own. The sight electrified the camp, but swirling clouds swiftly hid the climbers from view. When, 2½ hours later, Evans and Bourdillon reappeared at Camp 8, they were utterly exhausted and coated from head to foot in ice. They had turned back within 300 feet (91 meters) of the summit because they did not have enough oxygen to reach it and return safely.

Hillary and Tenzing were sure they could do better, and two days later they had their chance. Three other expedition members helped the men carry equipment to 28,000 feet (8,500 meters). Then they left the two men to sleep on a narrow ledge.

When they awoke, the tent was ferociously cold. They put on every stitch of clothing they had, and at 6:30 a.m., they set off for the summit.

Their route took them along the spine of the mountain through loose, unsafe snow. Both men sensed they were in great danger, but their determination drove them on.

By 9:00 a.m., they had climbed higher than anyone before them.

Suddenly, Tenzing was in trouble: He was gasping for breath. Hillary rushed to check the Sherpa's oxygen. Ice had blocked his mask, suffocating him. The horrified New Zealander flexed the rubber tubes to break the ice. To their relief, oxygen flowed again.

Hillary and Tenzing battled with exhaustion as they raced to reach the summit before their oxygen supplies ran out.

They pressed on, scrambling up a treacherous, icy crack to the final ridge. Frustratingly, a series of false summits hid the peak from view. As they reached the top of each one, another peak appeared ahead. The effort of cutting snow steps exhausted Hillary, and when he finally reached the top, his first reaction was to look for a further summit. There wasn't one.

Hillary was standing on the top of the world. Tenzing clambered up behind him. They had done it! The two men shook hands. Then, as the full realization of what they had achieved sank in, Tenzing joyfully embraced Hillary.

However, their limited supplies of oxygen meant they could not linger on the summit. Hillary took photographs and picked up a handful of pebbles as souvenirs. Tenzing, a Buddhist, made an offering of food to the gods of Chomolungma (the Tibetan name for Everest). Then the two mountaineers, soon to be the most famous men in the world, set off to rejoin their companions.

TENZING AT THE TOP
For Hillary and Tenzing, climbing Everest was a lonely triumph, but their success has made the mountain a crowded place. Today, tour companies guide wealthy trekkers to the summit. Litter lines the routes, and inexperienced climbers die in their rush to reach the top.

THE FIRST JOURNEY IN SPACE

The story so far…

On April 12, 1961, Gagarin woke before dawn and put on his spacesuit. He knew that his mission to orbit the earth was dangerous. No human had ever flown in space or experienced weightlessness before. Some doctors were unsure that he would even be able to swallow. When Gagarin's engineers wished him luck, some embraced him as if they might never see him again. After these emotional farewells, Gagarin climbed inside the spacecraft, and the countdown began.

THE FIRST COSMONAUT Yuri Alexeyevich Gagarin (1934–68) grew up on a farm in Russia (then part of the Soviet Union). As an apprentice engineer, he joined a flying club, and his skills as a pilot earned him a place at a military flying school. By the time he was 23, he was flying MIG-15 fighter aircraft. Two years later, he began training as a cosmonaut (Soviet space pilot). On April 11, 1961, he learned that he had been chosen to fly the world's first crewed spacecraft, Vostok, the following day.

INSIDE HIS CRAMPED CAPSULE, Gagarin was nervous. The launch procedure, familiar from months of training, had stopped abruptly. After an anxious wait, he heard a mission controller's voice in his headphones.

"Yuri, we have a small problem here. We're not getting the KP-3 signal to confirm that your capsule hatch is sealed. We're going to have to fix it."

It was a frustrating delay, but once the technicians had unscrewed and replaced the heavy hatch, the countdown continued. Gagarin felt the jolt as the launch tower pulled back. A roar far below told him that the gigantic rocket engines had ignited. The huge launcher—an adapted nuclear missile—shook and swayed as it thrust its way into the sky.

"Let's go!" Gagarin shouted excitedly.

He soared higher and higher: higher than anyone had ever soared before: 12 times higher than the highest-flying aircraft. The booster's increasing speed multiplied the G-force (the pull of gravity). It pressed Gagarin into his seat as if he were many times heavier than he was on the ground.

Just nine minutes after the launch, the rocket motors shut down. Now weightless, the cosmonaut could relax at last. Through his porthole, he saw planet Earth as nobody had ever seen it before.

"I can see the clouds," he told mission control. "I can see everything. It's beautiful!"

More passenger than pilot, Gagarin could do little except stare in wonder as he flew over the Arctic and across America's night sky.

His spacecraft was controlled from the ground. Unless something went wrong, he would not need to touch any of the controls. In fact, the single orbit was faultless, and after just 90 minutes, it was time to return. The retro-rockets fired, pushing the capsule toward Earth. The craft lurched wildly, and the instruments flickered and died—exactly as planned. But after a moment, they came back on again.

The capsule was behaving strangely. It was spinning and tumbling, like a toy airplane out of control. It was also getting dangerously hot.

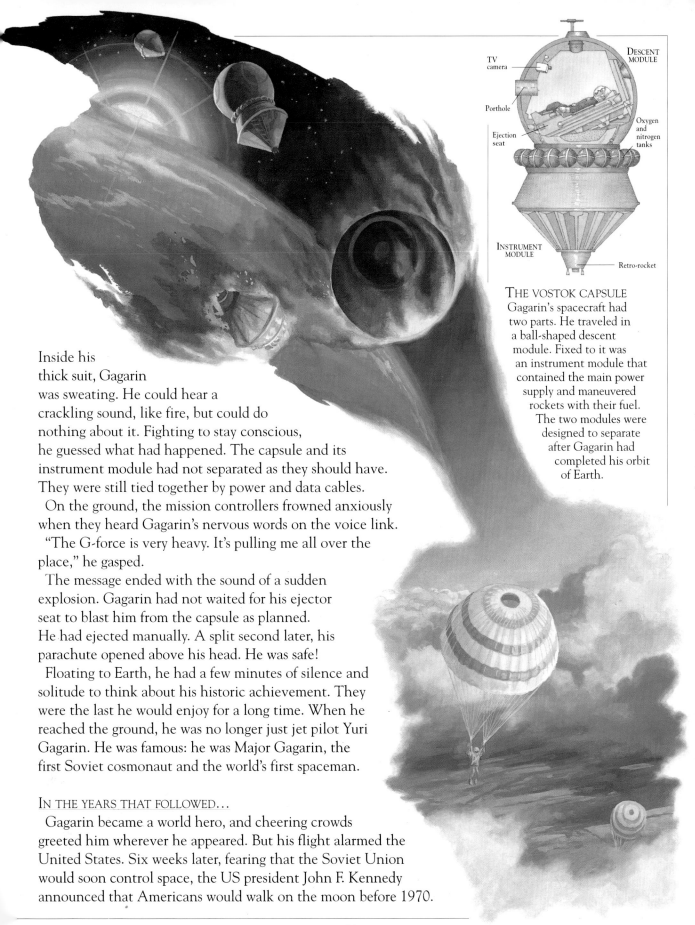

THE VOSTOK CAPSULE
Gagarin's spacecraft had two parts. He traveled in a ball-shaped descent module. Fixed to it was an instrument module that contained the main power supply and maneuvered rockets with their fuel. The two modules were designed to separate after Gagarin had completed his orbit of Earth.

DESCENT MODULE

TV camera

Porthole

Ejection seat

Oxygen and nitrogen tanks

INSTRUMENT MODULE

Retro-rocket

Inside his thick suit, Gagarin was sweating. He could hear a crackling sound, like fire, but could do nothing about it. Fighting to stay conscious, he guessed what had happened. The capsule and its instrument module had not separated as they should have. They were still tied together by power and data cables.

On the ground, the mission controllers frowned anxiously when they heard Gagarin's nervous words on the voice link.

"The G-force is very heavy. It's pulling me all over the place," he gasped.

The message ended with the sound of a sudden explosion. Gagarin had not waited for his ejector seat to blast him from the capsule as planned. He had ejected manually. A split second later, his parachute opened above his head. He was safe!

Floating to Earth, he had a few minutes of silence and solitude to think about his historic achievement. They were the last he would enjoy for a long time. When he reached the ground, he was no longer just jet pilot Yuri Gagarin. He was famous: he was Major Gagarin, the first Soviet cosmonaut and the world's first spaceman.

IN THE YEARS THAT FOLLOWED…

Gagarin became a world hero, and cheering crowds greeted him wherever he appeared. But his flight alarmed the United States. Six weeks later, fearing that the Soviet Union would soon control space, the US president John F. Kennedy announced that Americans would walk on the moon before 1970.

THE FIRST MOON LANDING

The story so far…

On July 16, 1969, the huge Saturn rocket blasted off, sending three astronauts into orbit around the Earth. Once in orbit, they locked together the landing craft, *Eagle*, and the command module, *Columbia*. Then they fired booster rockets to carry them the 240,000 miles (390,000 km) to the Moon. Four days later, they were in orbit around the Moon. Armstrong and Aldrin crawled into the *Eagle* and sealed the hatch. Their descent to the surface of the Moon began under computer control.

THE ASTRONAUTS
United States astronauts Neil Armstrong, Edwin "Buzz" Aldrin, and Michael Collins (all 1930–) were the three crew members chosen for the Apollo 11 mission to the Moon. It was to be the first time a person had stepped onto the Moon's surface. The three men had all flown war planes, either in combat or as test pilots, and they had all flown in space before. Michael Collins was to stay in the command module, orbiting the Moon, while the other two astronauts landed. The landing craft would touch down at a site called the Sea of Tranquillity—not an actual sea, but a flat, dry plain.

"YOU CATS TAKE IT EASY ON THE LUNAR SURFACE!" Michael Collins bid his friends a hearty good-bye. Then with a spurt of flame, the *Eagle*'s rocket engine fired to begin the descent. Inside the landing craft, Neil Armstrong scanned the instruments. His companion, Buzz Aldrin, compared the displays of the two onboard computers. Although this was their first flight in the *Eagle*, they had rehearsed it hundreds of times in a simulator on Earth. This time, the craters below them were the real thing.

Buzz began to read out loud the figures from the craft's displays. At 6,000 feet (1,800 meters) above the surface, Neil interrupted him.

"Program alarm!" He pointed at a yellow warning light.

Buzz and Neil's eyes darted to the digital display. It said the error was a "1202." They exchanged puzzled glances. They had not seen this error in training. Both knew that they had only a few seconds to decide whether to turn back or to continue the landing.

Circling high above in *Columbia*, Michael Collins grabbed his check list and began reading through it. What did an error 1202 mean?

Before Collins could find the code, he heard a calm voice from Mission Control on Earth, "Roger, we're go on that alarm."

The yellow light signaled that the onboard computer was struggling to keep up with its work. But it was safe for the *Eagle* to continue its descent.

More confident now, Neil Armstrong switched the controls from automatic to manual. For the final stages of the descent, he would fly their small, bug-shaped craft himself. Buzz checked their altitude (height).

"Four hundred feet…three hundred…two hundred," he called out.

He looked anxiously at the display that showed their speed and read this out too. The *Eagle*'s spindly landing legs could absorb small bumps, but the astronauts would be in trouble if they hit the ground too quickly.

By his side, Neil's hands tightened around the joysticks that controlled the craft's speed and position. He stared out through his porthole. Now he had a good view of the ground below, and he did not like the look of it. *Eagle* had overshot its carefully chosen landing site.

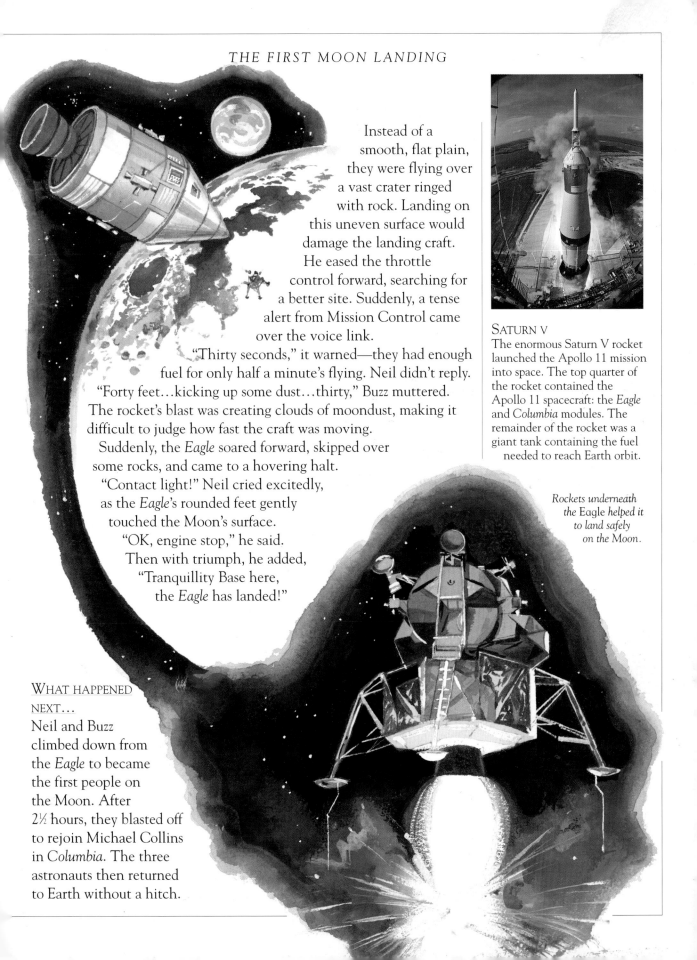

Instead of a smooth, flat plain, they were flying over a vast crater ringed with rock. Landing on this uneven surface would damage the landing craft. He eased the throttle control forward, searching for a better site. Suddenly, a tense alert from Mission Control came over the voice link.

"Thirty seconds," it warned—they had enough fuel for only half a minute's flying. Neil didn't reply.

"Forty feet…kicking up some dust…thirty," Buzz muttered. The rocket's blast was creating clouds of moondust, making it difficult to judge how fast the craft was moving.

Suddenly, the *Eagle* soared forward, skipped over some rocks, and came to a hovering halt.

"Contact light!" Neil cried excitedly, as the *Eagle*'s rounded feet gently touched the Moon's surface.

"OK, engine stop," he said. Then with triumph, he added, "Tranquillity Base here, the *Eagle* has landed!"

SATURN V
The enormous Saturn V rocket launched the Apollo 11 mission into space. The top quarter of the rocket contained the Apollo 11 spacecraft: the *Eagle* and *Columbia* modules. The remainder of the rocket was a giant tank containing the fuel needed to reach Earth orbit.

Rockets underneath the Eagle *helped it to land safely on the Moon.*

WHAT HAPPENED NEXT…
Neil and Buzz climbed down from the *Eagle* to became the first people on the Moon. After 2½ hours, they blasted off to rejoin Michael Collins in *Columbia*. The three astronauts then returned to Earth without a hitch.

INDEX

ACKNOWLEDGMENTS

The publisher would like to thank the following for their kind permission to reproduce the photographs:

a=above, b=below, c=center, l=left, r=right, t=top

AKG London: 12cl, 15br, 48–49, 50cl, 75cl, Erich Lessing 33br;

Ancient Art & Architecture Collection: 20cl;

Bridgeman Art Library, London / New York: *Portrait of Marco Polo (1254–1324)* by Dolfino Biblioteca Nazionale, Turin, Italy 14cl, Sloane 197 f.18 *Vasco da Gama (c.1469–1525)* British Library, London 23tr, *Hernando Cortés, the Spanish Conqueror of Mexico* (copy of an original) by Master of Saldana Giraudon/Museo National de Historia, Mexico City, Mexico 28cl, *Battle of Lepanto October 7, 1571* by Anonymous National Maritime Museum, London 8–9, *Don Quixote from Cervantes' "Don Quixote de la Mancha"* by Walter Crane (1845–1915) Private Collection 35tr, *Mr N. T. Hicks in the guise of the French highwayman Claude Duval (1643–70)* by English School Victoria and Albert Museum, London 38cl;

British Library, London: 62bl;

British Museum, London: 10cl, 23br, 30cl;

Jean-Loup Charmet: Societé de Geographie, Paris 58cl;

Christie's Images: 63br;

Corbis UK Ltd: Yann Arthus-Bertrand 59cr, Bettmann 80cl, Bettmann/Underwood & Underwood 79cr, Bettmann/UPI 90cl, ChromoSohm Inc/Joseph Sohm 54clb, Hulton-Deutsch Collection 73cr, Wolfgang Kaehler 41tr, Library of Congress 78cl, John Noble 67tr, Roger Ressmeyer 64br;

E.T. Archive: 36cl, 57tr;

Mary Evans Picture Library: 16cl, 34bl, 37br, 47tr, 60cl, 68cl, 71cr, 72–73, Fawcett Library 70cl;

Robert Harding Picture Library: 18tl, Robert Francis 66cla;

Hulton Getty: 40cl, 81tr;

The Kon-Tiki Museum, Oslo, Norway: 82cl, 85tr;

NASA: 92cl, 93tr;

National Maritime Museum, London: 25br, 41cl, 45tr, br, 71br;

Natural History Museum, London: 51tr;

Peter Newark's Pictures: 55tr, 56cl, 76cr;

Oxford Scientific Films: Richard Herrmann 84bl;

Royal Geographical Society Picture Library: 86cl, 88bl, tl, 89br;

Rye Town Hall: 39tr;

Statens Historika Museum, Stockholm: 13cr;

State Library of Victoria: La Trobe Picture Collection 69cr, tr;

Tony Stone Images: 17br, Jean-Marc Truchet 85br;

Topham Picturepoint: 46cl, National Library of Turin 32cl;

Michael Zabe: 31tr.

Jacket

AKG London: Erich Lessing back bc;

British Museum, London: front cla;

E.T. Archive: back trb;

Mary Evans Picture Library: back cr;

Hulton Getty: spine;

Royal Geographical Society Picture Library: front clb.

Dorling Kindersley would also like to thank: Sallie Alane Reason for the maps; Natasha Billing; James Briggs; Jayne Loader; Frank Love; Ken Nowell; Paul Roser (Old Melbourne Jail); and Terry L. Ross; also Chris Bernstein for the index; Anna Kruger, Alastair Dougall, and Martin Redfern for editorial assistance, Jacquie Gulliver, Peter Bailey, Amanda Carroll, Robin Hunter, and Anna Martin for design help.